FARRAR
STRAUS
GIROUX

Messages from My Father

Messages from

My Father

.

Calvin Trillin

Farrar, Straus and Giroux

New York

Copyright © 1996 by Calvin Trillin
All rights reserved
Published simultaneously in Canada by HarperCollinsCanadaLtd
Printed in the United States of America

Library of Congress Cataloging-in-Publication Data
Trillin, Calvin.
Messages from my father / Calvin Trillin.
p.   cm.
1. Trillin, Calvin—Family. 2. Authors, American—20th century—
Family relationships. 3. Russian Americans—Missouri—Kansas City—Social
life and customs. 4. Businessmen—Missouri—Kansas City—
Biography. 5. Fathers and sons—United States—Biography.
6. Kansas City (Mo.)—Biography. 7. Trillin, Abe. I. Title.
PS3570.R5Z469 1996   814'.54—dc20   [B]   95–47722 CIP

Portions of this book first appeared,
in somewhat different form,
in The New Yorker.

A leatherbound, signed first edition of this book
has been published by The Easton Press.

Photograph on page 81, by Alfred Eisenstadt, courtesy of Time Inc.
All other photographs courtesy of Sukey Fox or the author.

For Abigail Trillin and
Sarah Stewart Trillin—
precisely the granddaughters
Abe Trillin would have wanted

Messages from My Father

Chapter One

The man was stubborn. Take the coffee incident. This happened after I was living away from home, working as a reporter in the South. I was back in Kansas City for a visit, and my father and mother and I were sitting at the kitchen table. My mother had just made coffee. After pouring a cup for me, she asked if I wanted some milk in it.

"I don't use milk," I said.

"Well, I'll tell you one thing," my father said. "If you were blindfolded, you couldn't tell if there was milk in it or not."

As it happened, my father had never tasted coffee in his life. Was he a Mormon? No, he was not a Mormon. A health nut? No. The only nutritional theory I can remember his propounding was that you couldn't gain more weight from eating something than the food itself weighed, so devouring a one-pound box of intensely rich chocolate candy couldn't put on more than one pound. ("It stands to reason" was how he usually introduced that theory, among others.) Was he someone who had some rare allergy to coffee beans or caffeine? No, he thought of allergies as the sort of affliction that cropped up among my mother's relatives, who apparently constructed elaborate defenses against illnesses, real and imagined, and were described around our house as "nervous."

He didn't drink coffee because at some point in his childhood he had sworn that he never would. My father had sworn off any number of things. As a young man, he smoked for a few years and then swore off cigarettes. He swore off liquor before he was old enough to taste any—supposedly because of his disgust at the smell of stale beer in the taverns where he sold newspapers as a boy. As far as I can remember, he never gave any specific reason for swearing off coffee. It may be that coffee just got caught up in the boyhood oath against liquor, tossed in because it was also something grownups drank. I think he also must have sworn off swearing; if you ran him out of patience, his strongest expression was "For cryin' out loud!" I sometimes imagined my father as swearing off things just to keep in practice—the sort of person who looks at himself in the mirror after shaving one day and, for no particular reason, says to the image he sees, "You have hit your last bucket of driving-range golf balls" or "No more popcorn for you, young fella."

The act of swearing off, in other words, seemed to overwhelm whatever had triggered it. It's possible, I suppose, that over the years my father could have forgotten why he struck something off the rolls. In his case, though, forgetting what had been behind some absolute prohibition would not have been an argument for ending it. If he swore off something, it stayed sworn off. He had no need to offer explanations for the ban, because it applied to him alone. He didn't harangue people about the wickedness of demon rum; I have no reason to believe that he thought it was wicked. He had nothing against anyone else's drinking coffee, including me. He wasn't questioning my ability to tell the difference between black coffee and coffee with milk as a way of telling me that coffee wasn't worth drinking. He spoke in a perfectly agreeable tone, as if he were passing on some interesting fact about coffee that he had just read in the Kansas City *Star*.

I also spoke in a perfectly agreeable tone. I said, "Does it occur to you that, as someone who has never tasted coffee, with or without milk, you may not be a great authority on this subject?"

"I don't care what you say," my father said, using an opening phrase he often employed even if you hadn't said anything. "Blindfolded you wouldn't know if there was milk in it or not." This is stubborn.

My mother's view was that my father's stubbornness was perfectly understandable if you considered the family he came from. In my mother's conversations about relatives, just about everyone was permanently assigned one characteristic—usually a less than noble characteristic, like cheapness or slovenliness or a tendency to spoil children—that could be illustrated in one phrase. If I had inquired, while I sipped my coffee, about a relative I'll call Doris, my mother's reply would have begun, no matter what milestones had occurred in Doris's life since my previous visit to Kansas City, no matter what acts of kindness or charity Doris had performed, "You know Doris—sink full of dirty dishes." Whatever their individual characteristics, my father's relatives had been assigned the group characteristic of stubbornness. When the subject of the St. Joe people came up—my father had grown up in St. Joseph, Missouri, about fifty miles north of Kansas City, and when I was a child a lot of his relatives still lived there—my mother often summed up her feelings with one forcefully expressed word: "Mules!"

My mother accepted without question the notion that such characteristics as stubbornness run in families. In her mind, I think, it was partly a matter of what would now be called genetic predisposition. When I displayed behavior that she considered obstinate—that happened with some regularity—she would tell me that I took after my father's family, the St. Joe people. I was not troubled by this. There seemed to be only two alternatives, and what little boy wants to take after people who are nervous? When I got angry with my parents as a child, I stomped up to my room and remained there, silently smoldering, for periods that reflected impressive stubbornness—or so I thought until I read, many decades later, about a young man in Thailand who, denied a motorcycle by his parents, went to his room to sulk and was still there twenty-two years later. My mother also seemed to believe that the stubbornness of my father's family was, in effect, cultural: some tribes in New Guinea put rings in their noses; the St. Joe people practiced pig-headedness. She was perfectly willing to admit that her own mother's family had customs that encouraged nervousness. She nodded in confirmation when my father demonstrated the variety of their nervous gestures—a medley of tics and snorts that looked like something out of a Danny Kaye movie. It was she as often as my father who reminded us that some of her cousins drank a glass of warm water before retiring, to settle their stomachs.

I suppose I absorbed some of this belief in family characteristics, because when I found myself trying to figure out how my father's family became involved in the unlikely journey that took them to St. Joe in the first place, stubbornness was the first explanation I thought of. There was a lot about my father that was strictly western Missouri. He spoke with an accent that would be familiar to anyone who remembers the speeches of Harry S Truman. By his description, a golf drive that disappeared in the clouds or a towering home run that cleared the fence at Ruppert Stadium was "hit all the way to Clay County." A woman approaching middle age was "no spring chicken." A diminutive person weighed "seventy-five pounds soaking wet, with his boots on." It was from him that I picked up the not altogether elegant Midwestern phrase "I haven't had so much fun since the hogs ate my little sister." His childhood reminiscences were of St. Joe, around the time of the Great War; the one that stuck in my mind was that he had dislocated his shoulder jumping off a barn that once belonged to Jesse James, perhaps the best-known resident that St. Joseph, Missouri, has ever had.

But my father had actually been brought to St. Joe at the age of two, in around 1909. His family—then known as

Trilinsky—was from a place that was always described as "near Kiev." I've sometimes said that a child growing up in Kansas City, unfamiliar with the world of the shtetl, could get the impression that people who came from "near Kiev" had lived in the suburbs. Except that it would have had to be an extremely poor suburb—like one of those sorry, badly used farm towns which Midwestern cities sometimes envelop as they expand. I never heard the name of the place mentioned. I knew nothing of what life had been like near Kiev, or how the decision had been made to leave for a strange country several thousand miles away. It wasn't a secret. The people who knew—my grandparents' generation—simply didn't talk about it to me, maybe because I didn't ask. My father, of course, had virtually no memories of the Old Country to talk about. I asked him once if he remembered anything at all about Russia—that part of the world was referred to in my family as Russia, not the Ukraine—and he said that he had a vague memory of getting his foot stuck in the mud.

About all I knew of how my father's family got to St. Joe was that they went there directly from Galveston, Texas, where the boat from the Old Country had landed. When I was a child, I didn't realize that there was anything out of the ordinary in getting on a boat in darkest Europe, getting off in Galveston, Texas, and going straight from there to St. Joseph, Missouri. Only later did it occur to me that what I had learned in school about the great wave of immigration from Southern and Eastern Europe at the turn of the century said nothing at all about the route my family had taken from suburban Kiev to St. Joseph, Missouri—

the home of the Pony Express and, of course, Jesse James. Ellis Island was mentioned. The Statue of Liberty was mentioned. The Lower East Side was mentioned. There was not a word about Galveston, Texas. How did this family— a family indistinguishable from thousands of other poor Eastern European Jewish families saying their farewells to the czar, a family that could have been expected to fetch up on, say, Delancey Street—land in Galveston?

Could it have been stubbornness? According to one of the theories I came up with, my grandfather and his brother-in-law, my Uncle Benny Daynovsky, were talking to a friend of theirs one day in the suburbs of Kiev about where you land when you go to America. I knew that my grandfather and Uncle Benny went to America first, followed a couple of years later by my grandmother and my father and his older sister. In the conversation I imagined, the only two places any of the participants had ever heard of in America were New York and Texas. The friend said that when you went to America you landed in New York. My grandfather shook his head. "No," he said. "Texas." By the time they all actually left for the New World, my grandfather knew that the place you landed when you went to America was indeed New York, but he was willing to travel a couple of thousand miles out of his way in steerage rather than admit that he'd been wrong. Mules!

"In the grocery business it's accepted that one measure of a man's success is raising a son with enough sense to go into another line of work."

(TOP: EDYTH WEITZMAN TRILLIN STANDING WITH HER FATHER, BEN WEITZMAN. BOTTOM: ABE TRILLIN IN HIS FIRST GROCERY STORE)

Chapter Two

My father was a grocer. At least, that's what I always say when I'm asked what he did for a living. Actually, he got out of the grocery business when I was eleven or twelve. While I was in high school, he bought and ran a restaurant —a rather bland, boozeless place in a row of shops not far from where we lived. He changed its name from Hoover's to Trillin's. During that period, in the box marked "Father's Occupation" on those cards you had to fill out in block letters at the beginning of every school term, my sister, Sukey, and I wrote, with as much of a flourish as we could get out of block letters, "Restaurateur." He was briefly the part owner of a tavern, although I don't think he spent enough time there to catch the whiff of stale beer. He was, also briefly, the owner of a small residential hotel that, as I remember, bore the unlikely Kansas City name of La Palma—or maybe even *The* La

Palma. He was involved for a time as a partner in building a small subdivision. In the last years of his life, he worked in commercial real estate. Some of these enterprises overlapped, but, now that I've figured out the dates, I find, to my surprise, that he spent almost as many years doing other things as he spent in the grocery business.

Still, when I think of my father's work it's the grocer's constant, often monotonous routines that come to mind: the predawn trips to the city market, the six-day weeks, the regular inventories that ended with both of my parents sitting at the breakfast-room table operating adding machines, the imprecations against the chain stores that were trying to put independent grocers out of business. In an article that dealt partly with a man in Milwaukee who was for a time a second-generation grocer, I once wrote, "The grocery business is notorious for embodying just about every headache that exists in retail trade—dreadful hours that culminate in Saturday's being the busiest day of the week, endemic labor problems, spoilage. In the grocery business it's accepted that one measure of a man's success is raising a son with enough sense to go into another line of work." I must have been thinking of my father as well as of the man in Milwaukee, although I don't recall my father's having any labor problems beyond the contretemps that were presumably behind his theory—one of his absolute theories, leaving no room for exceptions—that a deep streak of insanity ran through people who earned their livings as butchers.

"Harold doesn't seem crazy to me," I remember telling him once about a butcher I liked.

The answer was the same as when I pointed out a cousin

of my mother's who did not appear to have any sort of nervous tic: "It just hasn't shown up yet."

My father was himself a second-generation grocer—his father, who died before I was born, had run a little grocery store in St. Joe—and he definitely thought of himself as someone with enough sense to go into another line of work. Patching together memories of vague references, Sukey and I think that some time between the time he graduated from Robidoux Polytechnic High School and the time he moved to Kansas City he may have been involved in an unsuccessful business venture in St. Joe. For whatever reason, going into a small business that he was already familiar with apparently became the only option that seemed viable. Before he had his own store, he was in partnership for a time with his cousin Jack. At least, I thought Jack was a cousin. When my mother was elderly, she jettisoned any number of relatives on my father's side of the family, the way some older people who have moved into more compact quarters shed excess furniture. I don't mean she stopped seeing them; she withdrew recognition of them as cousins. "How's Cousin So-and-so?" I might ask on a trip home, only to be told, "Those people were never related to us." Jack was one of the first to go over the side.

Particularly in those early days, when my father was trying to make a living from a tiny store on the edge of downtown Kansas City during the Depression, my mother worked alongside him, which made her a second-generation grocer herself. She often said that she had grown up in a grocery store. I have a photograph of her as a teenager, standing solemnly with her parents in one of those old-fashioned stores which displayed cans and boxes in perfect pyramids. Her father was still operating a little grocery store when I was a child. He was an extraordinarily sweet man named Ben who was called Pop not just by us but by my father's family and even by my friends and Sukey's friends. Apparently, sweetness was not always enough to keep a business going: I also have a picture of him in what seems to be a sort of soda shop and a picture of him next to some gas pumps under a sign that says "Ben Pays the Tax." When my mother said that she had grown up in a grocery store, it didn't mean that she played quietly in the corner while the grownups did the work. In the last years of her life, when she finally agreed that hiring a private aide at the nursing home was a worthwhile way to spend money she had worked hard for, the phrase she used to justify her decision was "Otherwise, why did I sack all those onions?"

Eventually, my father owned five grocery stores, almost any one of which would fit into, say, the dairy department of a modern Kansas City supermarket. Sukey and I could call them off, like a litany: Eighth and Tracy, Fifteenth and Broadway, Twenty-fourth and Lister, Thirty-first and Benton, Fifty-fifth and Paseo. The first four were known as City Food Stores. Fifty-fifth and Paseo, the newest and largest store, carried the modern name of Trillin's Super Market. Having five stores, each supposedly with its own manager, did not reduce my father's hours. It made for even more butchers. My mother still filled in often at the checkout counter, usually at Fifty-fifth and Paseo. It was a point of pride with her that she was the fastest checkout person my father had available. (Both she and my father, products of the era when grocers totted the bill on the back of a paper sack rather than at a checkout cash register, could add a column of numbers so quickly that it might have qualified as a parlor trick if most of the other people in the parlor hadn't themselves been grocers.) Even with five stores, my father got up at four in the morning six days a week to go to the city market for his produce. When people he met heard of this schedule, they almost always said to him something like, "Well, I suppose you get used to it after a while, don't you?" and he always said, "No." At some point, my mother began reminding him that other grocers truly managed all right by sending someone else to the market or even ordering produce over the phone. Trying to persuade him of that, she said, was "like talking to the wall."

My father hated the grocery business. When he began, he had registered a sort of time-release oath that called for him to leave the trade after a certain number of years. There was never any question of building a business that he might hand on to his son. It was a given in our family that my father was a grocer so that I wouldn't have to be. If his business had grown into a large supermarket chain instead of a handful of neighborhood grocery stores, the oath, I'm sure, would have still been in force. As it turned out, though, he wasn't able to meet his deadline. The pledge fell due during the Second World War, a force even more powerful than one of my father's oaths. When the war was over, he began selling his stores. In a year or two, they were gone. He was in his early forties.

Looking back on this, I see it as a move of astonishing audacity. Not that I ever doubted he would abandon the grocery business once the time-release oath came due. The man was stubborn. On the other hand, I think that even as an eleven- or twelve-year-old boy I must have understood that my father was a cautious businessman, someone with a storekeeper's dread of debt. We didn't even have a mortgage on our house. Living in a middle-class neighborhood in a middle-American city during the Second World War and the boom that followed it, I had literally never heard of someone's father not working. When my father was asked during the next year or two how he made a living, he sometimes said that he was able to support his family by playing pitch with his city-market cronies, whose workday began to slow up enough around nine in the morning to permit a game of cards. Sometimes the sucker mentioned was a cousin of ours who had moved to our block from Independence and the game was gin rummy.

My father was, in fact, skilled at cards. He played a lot of gin rummy, pitch, pinochle, poker—basically everything except bridge, which I'm afraid he considered a game that women play in the afternoon. Not that he disdained playing cards with women—or with children, for that matter. He played cribbage with one of his sisters, my Aunt Hannah. He played gin rummy and hearts with my mother and Sukey and me. Gin rummy was probably his favorite game. He had his own way of declaring gin—without speaking, he waved his index finger slowly back and forth, and then gently laid his cards on the table—and his own theories of gin strategy to discuss with regular opponents. One regular—a man named Phil Horowitz, who believed that the ultimate advantage lay with the player who kept his hand pared down—could express his own approach to gin rummy in a simple motto that always sounded to me like a philosophy of life for some of those men who knew that their stores had to run close enough to the bone to make it through bad times as well as good: lose less.

For a year or two, my father may well have been heading for a pitch game at the city market when he left the house, at about the same time that neighbors like Mr. Doty and Mr. Arnold and Mr. Cunningham were leaving for work, but his remark about making a living as a card shark was not meant seriously. He would never have played cards for stakes that might have had any effect on supporting a family of four. He would have considered that sort of gambling an act of shameless profligacy. I assume that my father's attitude toward money was formed partly by the Great Depression —he was in his early twenties when the crash came—but I can't remember much discussion of the Depression as a distinct era. He and virtually everyone he knew had been poor in the first place. He had prospered by working hard at least six days a week—days that began at four in the morning—and watching every penny. He wasn't stingy, but he was thrifty. He was the sort of man who preferred to stop for a bag of peanuts (the large economy size) on the way to the ballpark rather than pay what was being asked at the stadium for a tiny package. If he had hit it rich, he would have been one of those millionaires who are described in newspaper features as flying coach and being willing to drive a few blocks to get to a store that's having a special on paper towels. Because he thought his children should see the country, he organized summer automobile trips that lasted for weeks, but he'd wince every time Sukey ordered the most expensive item on the menu. (I was no problem in this regard, since I ate practically nothing but hamburgers.) Throughout his life, he seemed stunned by any price that was completely out of whack with what a prudent person could have been expected to pay in 1941. In the late sixties, a couple of years after my wife, Alice, and I got married, we decided that the way to find a place large enough to raise a family without leaving Greenwich Village was to look around for a brownstone that had a down payment we could manage and then rent out a floor or two in order to keep the mortgage-holder at bay. My father asked what such a building could be expected to cost. When we gave him an approximate figure—a figure that now, of course, seems rather modest—he responded with a Yiddish phrase that, I'm told, translates roughly into "It's going dark behind my eyes."

As a child, I understood that frugality was a matter of character but I had no idea whether or not it was also a matter of necessity. When my father sold his last grocery store, I had no way of knowing whether we could afford a lull in the breadwinner's efforts. He was not the sort of person who talked about such matters to children. My mother, of course, had worked off and on all her life, but not for other people; the possibility that she might work outside the family business was never in the picture. Looking back, I assume that the war had been a prosperous time for grocers and that my father had carefully put aside whatever funds were necessary to carry him through a period of look-ing for another line of work—just as he had carefully put aside the funds necessary before having our house built. Sukey and I weren't exactly worried, but we were at a loss as to how to describe our family's situation. What were we supposed to put in the space marked "Father's Occupation" on the cards we filled in with block letters at the beginning of each term? The two of us had a sort of meeting about that. What we decided on was "Temporarily Retired."

I continued to think of him as a grocer. I was out of college before I was able to walk into a Safeway or an A&P without a twinge of guilt. I still think of him as a grocer. Part of the reason may be that some of the values I associate with him are intertwined with the grocery business. He paid his bills the day he got them. He cared about the people who worked for him—even the insane butchers. Once, when he had to fire someone—the way he would have put it is that he "had to let someone go"—I happened to over-hear the conversation. I had been stocking shelves at Trillin's Super Market, and, at the end of the day, I was waiting for my father to finish up so we could go home. What I over-heard made me think that even if I could ever bring myself to fire someone I could never do it with that combination of firmness and what I would now call sensitivity—a word that, it almost goes without saying, I was unfamiliar with at the time. I always took it for granted that his strict notion of honesty was central to the way he ran his grocery stores, although at home it sometimes manifested itself in rules that seemed to approach the loony side of upright: a child who was small for his age not paying full adult fare at the movies a day after his twelfth birthday would be cheating the movie theater; a boy driving the day before his sixteenth birthday would be breaking the law. He raised me not to be him, I once wrote, but it has occurred to me more than once that a reporter could do worse than aspire to a standard of behavior reflected in my father's approach to being a grocer: give good weight, refuse to buckle under to pressure from the chain stores, treat with contempt the wartime temptation to get rich by cutting a few corners.

"He had his own way of declaring gin—without speaking, he waved his index finger slowly back and forth, and then gently laid his cards on the table."

"My father, I think, did not make a strong first impression."

Chapter Three

My father, I think, did not make a strong first impression. His name was unprepossessing. He was called Abe—not Abraham, just Abe—and he had no middle name or initial. For a while in later years—at the time, I suppose, when he worked in real estate and may have had a need for a business card—he called himself A. H. Trillin. I think that petered out when Sukey, who was always better at kidding him than I was, started calling him Ah-Ha! He was short, around five feet five. He had a prominent nose and a negligible chin and clear blue eyes. He was light-complexioned. He was strong—naturally thick in the chest and shoulders, I think, and probably made stronger by years of carrying heavy boxes around grocery stores. (He had a characteristic way of carrying a case of canned goods or a paste-board box full of groceries—on one hand, bent back near the shoulder, the way a waiter sometimes carries a heavy tray.) As a young man, he had wrestled at the Y. He admired strength. He often used the word "powerful," and when he did he wasn't talking about someone who was a titan of business or a man to be reckoned with at City Hall; he was talking about someone who could lift the end of a car off the ground.

When I was a child, I took it for granted, as children do, that my father was powerful in both senses of the word—as well as being a lot smarter than most other people. (Any time I needed confirmation of that, all I would have had to do was to ask him to add a column of figures.) He was the leader not only of our own family but of the family he had come from—an oldest son whose father had died at an early age. It was my father, I knew, who, a couple of years before I was born, had taken one of his brothers to the Mayo Clinic, the Lourdes of Midwesterners, for treatment of an illness that turned out to be beyond even the skills of the Mayo doctors. For a while, after the war, he employed his surviving brother, my Uncle Maish; for years, he employed one of his brothers-in-law. In a circle that began with his siblings and included some of the other St. Joe relatives, he appeared to be the most substantial and prosperous person.

I remember the moment when it dawned on me that my father did not impress the world at large as a powerful figure. We were at a camera store on the Plaza—a faux-Andalusian shopping district that remains the most elegant place for retail business in Kansas City. I don't remember how old I was, but it was old enough, at least, to be using a camera. We were standing at a counter waiting to be helped, but nobody seemed to be paying much attention. My father was standing quietly, with a faraway look in his eye, and it struck me that he was not one of the people in the world who would noisily demand service or one of the people whose very presence would command attention. He did not know people who would have then been called influential. He was not powerful in the way that word is often used— although I suspect that in those days he and Uncle Maish together might have gone a long way toward lifting the end of a car off the ground.

In novels of American strivers, the sort of realization I had in that camera store can cause the hero to become disillusioned with his father or to resolve that he himself will, at any cost, be a person who commands attention. I didn't have that sort of reaction. I do remember the moment—I remember the precise counter we stood at and precisely the direction we were facing—but it was not a moment that changed my opinion of my father or changed the way I thought about myself. That may have been because in his own world he was a figure of such strength. It may have been because his values were so deeply embedded—he had such stubborn confidence in their rightness—that it would have seemed trivial to put much weight on how the world of less certain human beings might respond to him.

Also, I understood that my father, who in some ways seemed so Midwestern, had a strong sense that proper behavior was modest behavior—the sense that Midwesterners reflect when they respond to an expression of gratitude or admiration by saying something like "No big deal." Even the words to live by that I have always associated most strongly with him—"You might as well be a mensch"— lack grandiosity. The German word *Mensch*, which means person or human being, can take on in Yiddish the meaning of a *real* human being—a person who always does the right thing in matters large or small, a person who would not only put himself at serious risk for a friend but also leave a borrowed apartment in better shape than he found it. My father clearly meant for me to be a mensch. It has always interested me, though, that he did not say, "You must always be a mensch" or "The honor of this family demands that you be a mensch" but "You might as well be a mensch," as if he had given some consideration to the alternatives.

I also knew that he had contempt for people who felt the need to pump up their own importance. The phrase he used to describe that sort of person was "big *k'nocker.*" The Yiddish word *k'nocker*, with both of its first two consonants pronounced, comes from the German word that means "to crack." Apparently, it referred originally to the boss who cracked the whip, and then evolved into a word that is, more or less, a derisive form of what Americans mean when they say "big shot." My father used it to refer to people who boasted of their triumphs or drove showy cars or displayed signs of having absorbed the teaching of the Talmud on the blessedness of charity without going on to read the section that says that the most blessed charity is the kind given anonymously. These were big *k'nockers*. The phrase has never left my consciousness. There have been occasions in New York when, for one reason or another, I have spent an evening in the apartment—always a luxurious, lavishly decorated apartment—of the sort of person who boasts about the art on the walls and drops a lot of names and makes sweeping pronouncements with an air of absolute infallibility. Going down in the elevator at the end of the evening, I can feel Alice looking at me. She knows what's going through my mind: I'm thinking about what my father's response to the evening would be. He would say nothing all the way down. As the elevator doors opened and we walked into the lobby, he would sum up the host in two words: "Big k'nocker."

My father was matter-of-fact about his belief that most people didn't leave a lasting impression. It was that belief, he said, that was behind his decision to wear only yellow neckties. This must have begun when I was in high school and my father was in the restaurant business. He said something about how most people don't stand out from the crowd, and how it helped to have a sort of signature. His was going to be yellow neckties. They wouldn't necessarily be solid yellow, but yellow had to be the basic color. It struck me as a pretty dumb idea—actually, somewhere between dumb and embarrassing. I didn't see the point of identifying yourself by the color of your necktie. What was so great about having someone say, "Oh, yes, Abe Trillin —the guy with the yellow ties"? I don't think I shared these reservations with my father. There may even have been an occasion or two in the ensuing years—a birthday, my return from a long trip—when I presented him with a yellow tie. The problem of what to get your parents as gifts is often so acute that sons and daughters will leap upon any hint of a hobby or a collection, relentlessly marking birthdays year after year with fishing flies or elephant statuary, long after the parent in question has grown tired of fishing or come to the conclusion that elephants are not as graceful-looking as he once thought. With my father, of course, there was no danger that, between birthdays, he had given up his pledge to wear nothing but yellow ties. He didn't give up pledges.

"It would no more have occurred to me to accompany my mother to a performance of 'Carousel' than it would have occurred to Sukey to go with my father to the Golden Gloves."

Chapter Four

When I was a child, I went to the city market
with my father once a summer. I remember shiv-
ering in the cold as I stood in the garage at four
in the morning—which is yet another example
of the vagaries of memory, since it has never been
even faintly cold in Kansas City in the summer
at any hour of the day or night. The trip to the
market was one of our annual rituals, the others
being the Golden Gloves amateur boxing tournament, the national small-college basketball
tournament, and the American Royal Livestock
Show. At the American Royal we covered all
livestock barns, doing a thorough inspection of
what I think was actually every single cow and
every single sheep and every single pig present.
My father was a methodical man. I never knew
exactly what we were looking for in our inspection tour, but I shared his satisfaction at the suc-
cessful completion of our rounds. I don't think

he had a strong interest in boxing or basketball; it was simply one of the things that fathers and sons in Kansas City did together, like playing catch or fishing or going to Boy Scout suppers. We did those things, too—although I have trouble focusing on the actual experience of fishing with my father, as opposed to the time we spent practicing our casting technique. The practice area he had chosen was the pond in a place called Loose Park—right alongside a busy street that led through an area of substantial houses from the Plaza toward our neighborhood. The pond was more or less ornamental. I was rather embarrassed to be casting large plugs into it, right there next to Wornall Road. It seemed to me that the people in passing cars could easily get the idea that we were dumb enough to be casting for large-mouth bass in the Loose Park pond. My father seemed oblivious to that danger.

At the city market, he was in his element. He may have never become accustomed to waking up at four in the morning, but he didn't seem at all tired when the repartee began. I've loved markets all my life. Whether the city is Veracruz or Tokyo or Dallas, I've often found myself just after dawn at the city market. It hasn't required intense analysis to understand the connection to those annual visits to the Kansas City market with my father. Once, as I walked through the Rialto market in Venice, I seemed to be experiencing a sense of well-being even stronger than I usually do on early morning market strolls. The scene was, in a way, exotic—boxes of squash with their blossoms still on were being unloaded from a barge; a fishmonger was humming an aria as he brightened up his display of Adriatic *rospi*, which have tiny teeth, by bending around an occasional fish's tail and hooking it into its mouth—but I heard myself mutter, "It's Kansas City." It had registered for the first time that the city market of Kansas City had seemed exotic to me partly because some of the people there were Italians. In general, the sort of European ethnic neighborhoods found in Eastern cities ended in St. Louis, on the other side of the state. Our high school, called Southwest to indicate its section of the city, had such a paucity of ethnics that we referred to a football player from my neighborhood as Guinea Gessler even though he argued—rather persuasively, I eventually decided—that he was in fact Swiss. My partner in a high-school comedy act sometimes did foreign accents, and years later I realized that he owed part of his success to the fact that not many people in Southwest High School had ever heard a foreign accent. But there was a small Italian neighborhood on the northeast side of town, and it must have provided a lot of the produce dealers at the city market. The people my father joked with had names like Jimmy Palermo. I can't remember the precise subject of their routines—I'd guess that they must have centered on ritualistic complaining about the quality and price of the produce—but I remember that they were as polished as the apples.

In the past I've described my father as shy, but I think that's not quite right. Although people tended to think of him as a man of few words, he was sometimes talkative, even in environments much less familiar than the city market of Kansas City. He had the Midwestern habit of chatting and joking a bit with waiters and sales clerks. He could pass an evening telling stories, particularly stories about the old days in the grocery business. He talked instantly and naturally to every child he ever met. He was shy in the sense that, like a lot of people, he found certain subjects difficult to bring up and he was uncomfortable talking about personal matters. When it came time for us to talk, father to son, about the mysteries of sex, for instance, he waited for an evening when he and my mother were going out, and just before they left he gave me a book on the subject—one of those old-fashioned books, as I remember, which talked in an obscure way about what seemed to be plant fertilization techniques. A few days later, he asked, rather awkwardly, if I had any questions; I said no, and gave him back the book.

So he didn't use the drive to the city market or the basketball game or the American Royal as an opportunity to talk things over with me. In fact, the drives often passed in complete silence. I don't think either of us considered that odd. We took it for granted that men were, by nature, stoic. Male and female roles were sharply divided in our house. I think that as a child I extended those roles beyond the four of us, considering my father's family vaguely masculine and my mother's family, with its penchant for glasses of warm water before retiring, vaguely feminine. The expectations for Sukey and for me were totally different. I was to be sent off to Yale, probably never to return. Sukey, after spending a couple of years at some state university that had a promising social life, was to get married and live in Kansas City, raising adorable children in convenient proximity to their grandparents. My mother and sister had their own ritual outings—concerts, road company performances of Broadway shows, shopping. It would no more have occurred to me to accompany my mother to a performance of *Carousel* than it would have occurred to Sukey to go with my father to the Golden Gloves.

Although I worked as a busboy in the restaurant, I was not involved with dirty dishes at home. Neither was my father. On rare occasions, he came home with a sackful of chestnuts and roasted them; otherwise, I wouldn't have thought that he knew how to turn on the oven. His only role in the preparing and serving and cleaning up of a meal was as commentator. After a few bites of, say, green beans, he'd stop to consider the taste—pausing in the almost scholarly way a serious devotee of fresh vegetables might pause these days before inquiring when the beans were picked— and ask the question he always asked: "What brand are these?" Sometimes my mother didn't know the answer. The mystery cans that had lost their labels at the grocery stores often found their way to our larder.

I suppose I thought of talk as womanly—chattering. Even when I was older, most of the words in any conversation I had with my parents were provided by my mother. When I phoned from college, my father's contribution, inserted in some brief pause, tended to be a phrase that was meant to wind down the conversation, like "Well, okay." I assume that was partly because he was calculating the cost of the call while my mother spoke. When I flew home for vacations and my parents picked me up at the airport, he said even less on the ride home. What I remember from those trips home is my father driving silently while my mother peppered me with questions I never quite got answered. Taciturnity is often thought of as a male trait in the Midwest, and the same, of course, is true in Jewish families. Talking about my parents years later, one of my relatives repeated his favorite Jewish joke: A struggling young Jewish actor announces to his parents one day that he finally got a part in a legitimate production. He is to play a Jewish father. His own father can't hide a look of slight disappointment. "What's the matter?" the actor says. "Of course, I'm proud of you, son," the father says. "But we were hoping you'd get a speaking part."

As a boy, I particularly associated women with talk about health. It seemed to me that my mother and her friends spent hours comparing complaints and doctors and complaints about doctors. My father must have consulted a doctor from time to time, but I never heard him mention it. Once, when I was a child, he gashed his head on a nail while he was getting the storm windows from a storage space above the garage; I can still remember where I was sitting when he came in the house, bleeding. Until then, I'm not sure it had fully registered on me that he was physically vulnerable the way other people were vulnerable. As I grew up, I never knew him to be sick, which is one reason that when I was called at college during my senior year and told that he'd had a major heart attack—he was forty-nine—I traveled to Kansas City thinking that it all had to be a terrible mistake. As he recuperated, he acknowledged that he had felt what must have been a smaller heart attack a couple of weeks before, while working in the yard. Naturally, he hadn't mentioned it to anyone; he was not a kvetch.

What strikes me as odd now is how much my father managed to get across to me without those heart-to-hearts that I've read about fathers and sons having in the study or in the rowboat or in the car. Somehow, the fact that he considered me a special case was understood from the beginning—a simple and powerful message that parents sometimes find it difficult to pass on to a child. Somehow, I understood completely how he expected me to behave, in small matters as well as large, even though I can't remember being given any lectures about it beyond that occasional, undramatic "You might as well be a mensch." Alice once wrote that throughout her childhood her parents sent her messages in code about values and expectations. It's possible that my father had a code so subtle that I didn't even notice its existence. Or maybe all this was distributed through my mother or my sister, either of whom would have treated a silent car ride as a sign that the other passenger was either sulking or expired. Maybe my father talked about these matters after all and I've forgotten the conversations, the way I've forgotten the sticky heat that is always present in Kansas City in the summer, even at four in the morning. If he did, it wasn't on those long early morning drives to the city market—about as far as you could drive in Kansas City, from the southwest corner to the other side of where downtown began, near where the Missouri River turned east and headed toward the Mississippi. I remember the silence. Once you let the silence build up on a trip like that, of course, it takes a lot to break it. I'm sure it never occurred to me that I might take the opportunity to tell my father how much I admired the way he had handled that firing at Trillin's Super Market.

Chapter Five

He was truly funny. He had a large collection of marching-band albums, and, when Sukey and I were children, there were times when one of them would set him to marching himself. This happened rarely and spontaneously; my father did not march on command. We would wait in one room while he circled the ground floor of our house. Every time he entered the room we were in, he would be marching in a different way—one time listing precariously off to one side, the next time rolling along in a Groucho Marx stoop, the time after that marching in a sort of hip-hop—pretending to take no notice of the fact that Sukey and I were both on the floor, helpless with laughter. In conversation with children who were not his own, he had some set routines. When he met someone who was studying a foreign language, he always asked for a translation of the same sentence:

"The left-handed lizard climbed up the eucalyptus tree and ate a persimmon." I have continued to use that sentence from time to time—I have some set routines myself, some of them his—and I have to say that the responses do not build confidence in the level of language instruction in this country. He also had a special word that he challenged any schoolchild to spell. It was, phonetically, "yifnif." I can present it only phonetically, because I never learned how to spell it.

Many years later, after I had mentioned "yifnif" in print, I was informed that Milt Gross, a humorist who captured the Yiddish accents of his characters phonetically, sometimes wrote about a woman named Mrs. Yifnif. It wouldn't surprise me to learn that my father, who loved dialect humor, had read Milt Gross's work. I can picture him chuckling over the beginning of a letter Mrs. Yifnif sent to her son's school principal in Gross's *Nize Baby*, published in 1925: "Mine Joonior hinforums me wot yasterday hefternoon in de school one from de pyoopills trew on heem a speetz-ball. So mine Joonior, wot he ain't, denks Gott, a cowitt, trew heem beck a speetz-ball wot de odder goot-fornotting docked so it flew gredually de speetz-ball de titcher in de faze." If Mrs. Yifnif did put the word in my father's mind, though, that association and that spelling had faded away. In my father's version, "yifnif" had no meaning. It existed only to be spelled.

Or to defy efforts at spelling. I once wrote a story based on the attempts to spell "yifnif" made by a carful of Boy Scouts on those occasions when my father drove us to a meeting. He always offered an array of prizes for the correct spelling, and in the story I mentioned as many as I could remember: a new Schwinn bicycle, a trip to California, a lifetime pass to Kansas City Blues baseball games, free piano lessons for a year, a new pair of shoes. I can't imagine that any of us would have been interested in free piano lessons for a year, but we made attempt after attempt to spell "yifnif" anyway:

"Occasionally some kid in the car would make an issue out of yifnif's origins. 'But you made it up!' he'd tell my father, in an accusing tone.

" 'Of course I made it up,' my father would reply. 'That's why I know how to spell it.'

" 'But it could be spelled in a million ways.'

" 'All of them are wrong except my way,' my father would say. 'It's my word.' "

There was, I knew, no chance that my father could have simply called any spelling we came up with wrong and thus avoided handing out the prizes; as I said in the story, "His views on honesty made the Boy Scout position on that subject seem wishy-washy." I never had any doubt in my mind that there was one correct way to spell "yifnif" and that my father knew what it was and that anyone coming up with it would get every single prize that had been offered.

I was convinced that he had in mind some enormously complicated spelling of what sounded like an extremely simple word. In the story, we wily Boy Scouts brought in a ringer—my cousin Keith, from Salina, Kansas, who had reached the finals of the Kansas state spelling bee. I really do have a cousin Keith who got to the finals of the Kansas state spelling bee—his mother was my Aunt Hannah; his father, my Uncle Jerry Cushman, was at that time the city librarian of Salina—but Keith never came with us to Boy Scout meetings and he doesn't know how to spell "yifnif." I've asked him. The fictional Keith's try was Y-y-g-h-k-n-i-p-h. At some point, I had become certain that "yifnif" began with a double "y"—"y" used as both a consonant and a vowel. I can't imagine what made me so sure of that. My father didn't give hints. As you were picking your way through the first syllable, he never said anything like, "You're doing fine so far." You tried to spell "yifnif," and when you were through he said, "Wrong." On the way to Scout meetings, when other boys in the car were waiting their turn to take a flier at winning a new pair of shoes, he'd say, "Wrong. Next."

He was a collector of curses, particularly old Yiddish curses of the may-you-have-an-itch-where-it's-impossible-to-scratch variety. Once, while he was visiting Alice and me in New York, he came back to our apartment with an addition to his collection which he had unexpectedly bagged on the Lower East Side. He had been in Katz's Delicatessen, where sandwich-makers stand above the crowd behind a long counter, piling on pastrami and maintaining a strict form of queue discipline ("And who are you—a movie star maybe?"). My father put in his order with the sort of little joke he might have used with a waiter in Kansas City. "Give me a corned beef sandwich," he said. "Make it lean, and I'll recommend you to the boss." The sandwich-maker looked down at him and said, "The boss! May the boss's nose fall off!" Washington Avenue in South Miami Beach was where my father expected to find curses. Sometimes known as Yenta Alley, it had grocery stores that had become the central battleground in South Florida for daily wars of nerves between the proprietors and retired Jews whose resources consisted of small fixed incomes and extensive experience in negotiating with the butcher. Yenta Alley in South Miami Beach is to collectors of curses what the Serengeti is to connoisseurs of lions. My father liked listening to the arguments even when they didn't contain curses. It was in a grocery store on Washington Avenue that he collected his favorite curse: an elderly woman shouted at a butcher, "May you have an injury that is not covered by workmen's compensation."

After loitering in the grocery stores on Washington Avenue for a while eavesdropping on arguments, my father sometimes went to the beach with his old 16 millimeter movie camera and took a reel or two that consisted entirely of fat women approaching the ocean. When it came to a willingness to traffic in humor that would now be seen as demeaning to women, he was not ahead of his time. If the subject of what to look for in a wife came up, for instance, he always raised the question of teeth. Occasionally, one of the young salesmen who came into Trillin's restaurant for lunch would announce that he was engaged to be married. "Abe," the salesman would say, as I imagine the scene, "I have met the girl of my dreams, my true love, the woman who was meant for me. I have asked her to be my wife, and—thank God, because I cannot live without her—she has agreed. We are engaged to be married."

"Did you check her teeth?" my father would reply, before he even offered his congratulations. One of his antic theories

"He referred to many animals he ran across—occasionally including a fish he'd caught—as Fred."

was that flaws of personality or looks or background could be corrected or adjusted to but bad teeth represented a life-long financial drain that could undermine the strongest union.

My father liked names. When he told stories to small children, there was often a character whose name sounded like Stoolie-allahmalochas. His version of Joe Blow was someone named Schlayma Puch, whose last name rhymed, more or less, with "shnook." He handed out names to real people, and some of them stuck. His name for my mother's first bridge-and-gossip set was the Clique Adorables. Eventually, my mother called them that, too. One of his friends was a small, cigar-smoking man we called Little Stuff Silverstein. He referred to many animals he ran across—occasionally including a fish he'd caught—as Fred. He got fancy, though, with the name of the only pedigreed dog we ever owned—a lazy, rather dim English bulldog. Although we referred to the dog as Buck, the name on his papers had been Sir Lancelot. My father, not considering that quite grand enough, extended it to Sir Lancelot O'Pujilus.

I believe that for my father the perfect anecdote would have featured a man with a funny name who finds himself in an embarrassing situation. The stories he told about old days in the grocery store leaned heavily on the humor that comes from someone backing into something that isn't what he thinks it is—the most ribald word I ever heard my father use was "goosey"—or of being frightened by something that turned out to be harmless. He enjoyed teasing people. When I was a little boy, he teased me about a temporary but intense devotion I had to Gene Autry, the singing cowboy—a devotion I would make some lame attempt to justify if I could remember anything about my hero except for the sponsor of his radio show, Doublemint chewing gum, and the name of his theme song, "Back in the Saddle Again."

He liked Jewish humor. We had some record albums by Jewish comedians that my parents and their friends found enormously entertaining and I found enormously frustrating. A long buildup that was at least partly in English always ended in a punch line—an uproarious punch line, judging from the response in my living room, and, I always suspected, an off-color punch line—that was inevitably delivered in Yiddish and thus lost on me completely. Like a lot of people from Eastern European Jewish backgrounds, he found Litvaks—Jews from Lithuania—such a rich source of humor that the word alone made him smile. My mother's family had come from Vilna—or near Vilna, really; their village was called something like Munchnik—and my father sometimes seemed to imply that their peculiarities had something to do with their Litvak origins. I was never quite sure what was so funny about Litvaks—I'm not sure now, even though I, too, tend to smile when I hear the word—but I accepted the fact that Litvaks were figures of fun as one of the elements that separated my mother's family from the band of stubborn Kiev suburbanites I identified with.

A lot of my father's own humor was strongly Midwestern. The joke I heard him tell more than any other was about a man who, traveling along a country road, sees a boy lying in the shade of a tree with a piece of grass in his mouth and his hat pulled down over his head. "Boy, if you can show me a lazier act than that, I'll give you a dime," the man says, and the boy replies, "Put it in my pocket." Once, when I was trying to describe Midwestern play-dumb humor, I used the real example of my father's visit to Tiffany's when he was in New York visiting Alice and me. He and my mother and Alice and I were standing at the counter, looking at something like silver pins, when he said to the salesman, "What's the name of this store again?"

"Why, Tiffany's, sir," the salesman said.

My father said that he had never heard of it, and asked if it had just opened. "I'm from Kansas City," he added, by way of explanation.

"Oh, no, sir," the salesman said. "It's been here for a number of years. It's quite a well-known store."

"Does it have anything to do with Cartier's?" my father asked. "I've heard of Cartier's."

"No, sir," the salesman said. "Nothing at all to do with Cartier's."

"Tiffany's," my father said, rolling the word around as if testing how it might work out as a name for a jewelry store. "Tiffany's. Well, that's a new one on me."

"The Old Country—untalked about, basically unexperienced by anyone in our immediate family—was a constant in our lives."

(TOP LEFT: ABE AND SADIE TRILINSKY. TOP RIGHT: ANNA TRILINSKY AND HER FIRST THREE CHILDREN. BOTTOM: THE TRILINSKY FAMILY IN ST. JOSEPH; ABE IS IN THE SECOND ROW, RIGHT)

Chapter Six

It seems to me that upbringings have themes. The parents set the theme, either explicitly or implicitly, and the children pick it up, sometimes accurately and sometimes not so accurately. When you hear people talking about their child-hoods, you can often detect a theme. The theme may be "Our family has a distinguished heritage that you must live up to," or "We are suffering because your father deserted us," or "No matter what happens, we are fortunate to be together in this lovely corner of the earth," or "There are simply too damn many of us to make this thing work." Sometimes there is more than one theme. It's possible, for instance, for an upbringing to reflect at the same time "We are suffering be-cause your father deserted us" and "There are simply too damn many of us to make this thing work."

When I was a child, I was under the impression that one of the themes of my upbringing was one of the grand American themes: "We have worked hard so that you can have the opportunities we didn't have." It's a grand theme partly because in its purest form it requires a suppression of ego: it requires people to think of their lives as taking meaning largely from being a transition to other people's lives—their children's. Thinking back on it, though, I realize that I might have misread the signals slightly. I think what was actually being presented was the immigrant subsection of that theme: "We have worked hard so that you can have the opportunity to be a real American."

Our immediate family would not have struck anybody as foreigners. The fact that my father had been born in the Ukraine seemed almost a technicality. My parents had Midwestern accents, even though they both happened to be fluent in Yiddish. We didn't live in an immigrant neighborhood; I suspect that a lot of the people I went to school with had grandparents who lived on the farm or in the small towns of eastern Kansas or western Missouri. But the Old Country—untalked about, basically unexperienced by anyone in our immediate family—was a constant in our lives. My mother was born in Kansas City, but her parents were immigrants. Her father, Pop, had one of those bone-chilling immigration stories often heard among people of that generation. Having, according to his account, evaded conscription by two or three different armies, he sailed to America as a teenager, scheduled to be met at the boat by a half brother. The half brother wasn't there. Pop looked around for him, but couldn't find him. He never found him. He never found anybody else he was related to—although, because his name was Weitzman, he sometimes referred to the founding president of the state of Israel as "my cousin Chaim."

I associated St. Joseph, where we showed up regularly on Sunday excursions to visit my father's family, not with the Pony Express or Jesse James but with immigrants who lived in the back of tiny grocery stores and responded to our arrival by running to the shelves for candy to press on Sukey and me. These were my father's aunts and uncles. I could never keep them straight, except for Uncle Benny Daynovsky, whom I remember as having a sort of magical connection with children. (One of my daughters met a roomful of my St. Joe relatives when she was maybe eighteen months old, and after one look at Uncle Benny—a funny-looking little man, then in his eighties—she walked right over and crawled up into his lap.) Sukey and I called one of our greatuncles Pruneface, after a scary-looking character in *Dick Tracy*, and for years I assumed Pruneface was Uncle Schroelik. That sounded like the sort of name a Pruneface look-alike would have. Schroelik, Sukey informed me long after I had grown up and moved away from home, was another name for Uncle Earl, who didn't resemble a *Dick Tracy* character at all. My father's mother, who remained in St. Joe during part of my childhood, struck me as the most impenetrably foreign relative of all.

Virtually everybody one generation older than my parents on both sides of my family spoke English with a heavy accent. By chance, the only other old person I saw regularly when I was about five also had an accent; the grandmother of the Doty kids, who were our best friends in the neighborhood, was a Norwegian American from Nebraska. I remember being astonished in first grade when I stopped on the way home from school for some milk and cookies at David Miller's house: his grandmother had gray hair and a grandmotherly air, but she spoke the way David and I spoke. It had somehow escaped me that there were elderly people who could speak regular English.

I eventually found out how the St. Joe people got to St. Joe. This discovery came after I was grown and married. Alice and I were on vacation in the Caribbean. Someone I'd met in the South, Eli Evans, had sent me a copy of *The Provincials*, his book on Southern Jews, and I was reading it on the beach. I had reached a passage on the tense relations at the turn of the century between the German Jews in New York—many of whom had become established, respectable businesspeople—and the horde of impoverished Eastern European immigrants pouring into the Lower East Side. It said, "The silk-hat banker Jacob Schiff, concerned about the conditions on the East Side of New York (and embarrassed by the image it created for New York's German Jews), pledged half a million dollars in 1906 to the 'Galveston Project,' which helped direct more than ten thousand East European immigrants through Galveston." In order to disperse the immigrants, Evans explained, arrangements were made for jobs in various parts of the South and lower Midwest. It all made sense. My family had, in fact, gone to St. Joe specifically to work in a cabinet factory run by a German-Jewish family—a line of work soon abandoned for storekeeping by just about everyone except for my Uncle Benny Daynovsky, who apparently rather liked making cabinets. The Trilinskys and the Daynovskys were obviously Galveston Project people. Years after I'd learned that, a man in California named Alan Wachtel, who had heard me mention my family's origins, was kind enough to go through microfilm of the records kept by the Galveston Project and send me copies of the relevant immigration documents—manifests of alien passengers arriving at the port of Galveston. There it was, in tiny longhand. The manifest of the S.S. *Köln*, arriving on October 5, 1907, from Bremen, listed my grandfather as Kussiel Trilinski, a thirty-one-year-old joiner (meaning carpenter, not someone who is almost certain to become a member of both Kiwanis and the Rotary) from a village that Wachtel eventually deciphered as Sokol'cha, a place about seventy-five miles west of Kiev. On March 10, 1910, the S.S. *Frankfurt* landed in Galveston with a complement of passengers that included my grandmother and two small children—Scheindel, my Aunt Sadie, and Abram, who in America became Abe, my father.

When I read Eli Evans's book on the beach that day, Uncle Benny may have been the last survivor of my grandparents' generation—a man in his late eighties who spent a lot of time tending his tomatoes in the yard behind his little row house in a part of St. Joe that I always remember as looking as if it had got frozen in place in around 1922. I sat up on the beach. "Embarrassed!" I said to Alice. "Who is Jacob Schiff to be embarrassed by my Uncle Benny Daynovsky!"

That was the first line of a piece I wrote about the discovery. My research consisted partly of coming up with embarrassing facts about the Schiffs, which did not prove terribly difficult. According to Stephen Birmingham's book *Our Crowd*, for instance, Jacob Schiff had displayed on his office walls two of the largest checks he ever wrote, one of them for $62,075,000. (Big *k'nocker*!) In the piece, I remind my wife that the *New York Post* survived one battle of the New York tabloid wars because its owner, Dorothy Schiff, had finked on the other publishers in the New York Publishers Association and settled with the union separately. (" 'Since when did you become such a big defender of the New York Publishers Association?' my wife said. 'My Uncle Ben Daynovsky never finked on anybody,' I said.") Acknowledging that my family in St. Joe had a certain local renown for stubbornness, I maintain in the piece that there was nevertheless nothing embarrassing about them. (Although my mother did not object to this statement, she might have quietly disagreed: at the time she met my father, I had often heard her say, some of the St. Joe people were so poor and benighted that their toilet paper supply came from the little pieces of tissue that oranges used to be wrapped in when they arrived at a grocery store.) Unlike Jacob Schiff, I point out, my Uncle Benny had never consorted with robber barons like E. H. Harriman ("When it comes to rapacious nineteenth-century capitalism, my family's hands are clean") and would have never put a framed check on his wall. (I did not go into the question of whether or not Uncle Benny actually had a checking account.) When I saw the St. Joe people at a wedding in Kansas City, I told them that I was working on the piece and hoped to

have it published somewhere before Uncle Benny's ninetieth birthday party.

"Don't mention his name," Uncle Benny's son said. "The
Russian army is still looking for him."

The Russian army, the Cossacks—all that was far enough
away to be material for jokes. We lived on a pleasant street
in a city then known as the Heart of America. My father
mowed the lawn, just the way Mr. Doty and Mr. Arnold
and Mr. Cunningham mowed the lawn. On summer evenings, we caught lightning bugs or we played croquet or
kick the can in the Dotys' backyard. We brought our meat
loaf to the covered-dish suppers that my Cub Scout pack
held regularly at the Broadway Methodist Church—although it is also true that my mother told us to stay away
from everyone else's meat loaf, on the theory that you could
never tell what "they" put in it. (This warning, I think, did
not grow out of her fear that we might find ourselves eating
trayf—she cheerfully cooked the bacon on family picnics
at Shelter House #4 in Swope Park—but out of an unfo-
cused suspicion about how Gentiles lived. She may have
suspected that Gentile meat loaf was adulterated not just
with pork but with filler or maybe even Jim Beam.) When
the time came, Sukey and I went to a high school that had
a strong resemblance to the high schools in the sort of
Hollywood movies that featured Andy Hardy—or, as it
turned out, the sort of movies that featured Paul Newman
and Joanne Woodward, since Southwest was the school
attended by the children of Mr. and Mrs. Bridge. After our
family had a dog named Buck, we had a dog named Spike.

I took it for granted that we were as American as anyone else.

I believe now that my father never took it for granted. It was my father, not his parents or some immigration officer, who changed the family name. I think we lived in that neighborhood precisely because it was where regular middle-class Americans lived. It was a vast section of southwest Kansas City that had been developed largely by a man named J. C. Nichols. He called it the Country Club District. The full name of the shopping district we called the Plaza is the Country Club Plaza, unless it's "the world-famous Country Club Plaza." The baccalaureate service accompanying our high-school graduation was actually in a house of worship called the Country Club Christian Church. Although there were eventually plenty of Jews in the Country Club District, there was a widespread feeling in the late thirties that its developer held the prevailing country club views on how few Jews it took to be too many. Just to be safe, my father had bought the land our house was built on through a Christian acquaintance—a salesman who called on him at the grocery stores.

A writer I know, Victoria Redel, has published a book of connected short stories, *Where the Road Bottoms Out*, about someone growing up in a comfortable suburb of New York in a family of cosmopolitan Jewish refugees, some of whom had made stops along their way in places like Belgium and Constantinople and Mexico. Most of the stops presumably ended badly, and it is assumed by the adults in the book that America, however comfortable and however tolerant, is just another one of these stops. The narrator expresses this in a way that sums up Jews as wanderers in one sentence: "In the easy suburban evenings our parents waited for our American disaster." When the daughters of the family in the book engage in some conventional suburban activity like marching with the school band, their father says to them, "You are not American." He says it, the narrator reports, "the way we heard other fathers tell their children not to run out into the street." When I read that, it occurred to me that my father's message, delivered with such assurance that it did not require articulation, was precisely the opposite: "You are American." It never occurred to him that the Trillins were going anywhere. There weren't any exotic ports of call behind us—just those Kiev suburbs— and there weren't any in our future. We were in America to stay.

I think my father dreamed of my going to Yale partly because that's where he believed the ideal American boy would go. It was all right there in a heroic novel he had read as a boy in St. Joseph—*Stover at Yale*. The longest argument my father and I had during my childhood was over the question of whether I was going to join the Boy Scouts. I didn't want to be a Boy Scout. My father wanted me to be a Boy Scout. American boys were Boy Scouts. I remember the argument as lasting for days, but maybe it just seemed that long. I argued, among other things, that I was being treated unfairly: how come Sukey, who was a year ahead of me in school, hadn't been forced to be a Girl Scout? I considered that a brilliant point, but it was, of course, based on my misreading of the theme that guided our upbringing. I might as well have asked why Sukey wasn't expected to go to Radcliffe or Wellesley. Sukey wasn't the American being fashioned here; I was. I became a Boy Scout—not an enthusiastic Boy Scout, perhaps, but a Boy Scout. I thought I had put up a pretty good argument, but I was, after all, only the second stubbornest person in the house.

My father had an American's optimism—the sort of quiet confidence about the future that was not always easy to find among the immigrants or first-generation Americans of that era. The people who came to this country in the great wave of immigration from Southern and Eastern Europe may have looked on America as the land of opportunity, but their experience over generations in the Old Country must have told them that they would be doing well to keep their heads above water. One part of them was waiting for their American disaster. A friend of mine—Joseph Machlis, a musicologist and writer and translator of operas—grew up an immigrant on the Lower East Side at precisely the same time my father was growing up in St. Joseph, Missouri. He says that at the close of the Passover seder, at the moment when it was traditional in Jewish homes to offer in the final prayer the phrase "Next year in Jerusalem," his father would push back from the table and say, in Yiddish, *"Iber a yor nischt erger"*—"Next year no worse."

In the immigrant community of that generation, pessimism and fearfulness were endemic. They were compounded by a conviction common among Jews that no Gentiles could be trusted. When I was in college, a Jewish friend's father—a cultivated man who had left Europe just ahead of the Nazi invasion of his country—often told his son and me that we were naïve to think that we would not be abandoned by our Gentile friends if one of them ever had to choose between us and his own people. My mother came from a background marginally more sophisticated than my father's. She had a regular American name from the start—Edyth. She occasionally mentioned, with some pride, that she was "not from Independence Avenue," where, apparently, the poorest Jewish immigrants in Kansas City had lived. Among the cousins in her generation of the family were college graduates and even doctors. The patriarch who had come to Kansas City from Lithuania in the previous generation was himself referred to as Dr. E.L.— although I suspect his medical credentials would not have borne serious scrutiny. Even so, my mother had more than a trace of the immigrant's fearfulness.

My father seemed to have no trace at all. He feared no pogroms. He saw no limitations. Although my parents' circle of friends was totally Jewish, it would have never occurred to him to question the long-term loyalty of my Gentile friends. He would have considered all of that kvetching. My father did not kvetch—about his health or his childhood or his business. (As a teenager, I sensed that the subdivision he was involved in, which was eventually completed at a modest profit or loss, was having some difficulties, but decades passed before I learned that for a while it had drawn us close to a financial catastrophe.) He did not expect kvetching from us. We always had close at hand an unadulterated example of the old shtetl outlook that my father clearly intended us to be absolutely free of—my mother's mother, who was beyond nervous. She might be described as somewhere between a person of great anxiety and a hysteric. I actually didn't much like her. Among other things, she always referred to my dog, Spike, as the *hundt*. When I complained about that, my mother assured me that *hundt* simply meant dog in Yiddish, but I knew that my grandmother didn't like Spike, or anything else suspected of not having the hygienic standards of her own kitchen sink. I knew that if she had anything good to say about Spike she would have referred to him in a language I understood. Years after I had left Kansas City and years after my grandmother had died, I went back home for a ninetieth birthday party we gave for her husband, Pop, whom I adored. After everybody left, and Pop and I were sitting alone, he began to talk about the days when he was a young man, living in Leavenworth, Kansas. "I was just a greenhorn," Pop said. All of his stories about his early days in America included the phrase "I was just a greenhorn." Pop told me that a man he knew in Kansas City, Dave Ginsberg, had mentioned a sister who was marriageable and had a five-hundred-dollar dowry. By chance, Pop had already met the sister in question, and already thought that she was someone worth pursuing. "That was your Uncle Dave, and his sister was your grandma," Pop said.

There was a long pause. I assumed that the story was over. "That's a nice story, Pop," I said.

Then Pop said, "They never paid me the five hundred dollars."

I told Pop that I'd like to help him collect the money but it was hard to think of anybody to dun. Uncle Dave, an optometrist who was my grandmother's eldest brother and leader of her family, had been gone for twenty years. I was also thinking, I have to admit, that five hundred dollars, even in turn-of-the-century funds, was not a lot to pay to get my grandmother out of the house.

The incident that, for our family, symbolized my grandmother's approach to life took place when I was in high school. She and my mother were at the hospital one day to be with Pop, who was having a minor hernia operation. Her blood pressure was presumably already at a level that might be discussed at a medical-convention seminar on the astonishing symptoms that can be provoked by stress alone. Then my father phoned my mother to say that Sukey had a bad stomachache and was coming in to the hospital, where she would probably have her appendix removed. When my grandmother was informed of this coincidence in the timing of medical procedures, her response was immediate and completely characteristic. She said, "Give me poison!"

"On those trips, my father, a man who during the rest of the year couldn't bear to delegate even the task of getting up at four in the morning to buy produce, went for weeks without calling Kansas City to check on the stores. He was on vacation."

Chapter Seven

Even before the war our family had taken a couple of long automobile trips in the summer—one all the way to California—and the custom was revived as soon as gas rationing ended. In the years after the war, one of the gasoline companies, Conoco, began offering a large, spiral-bound book of maps put together especially for an individual customer's automobile trip. A thick black line ran along the highway that Conoco's travel experts were suggesting as the best route. The book was called, I think, a Touraide. My father always ordered one. Except for one trip we took to the East Coast, the black line in our Touraide led west toward California. Our routes varied with each sweep across the continent so that we could take in the sights that my father thought Sukey and I should see. I still remember standing deep inside the Carlsbad Caverns when the guide turned out the light so that we could see what pure darkness was. I remember the rustic cabins in Yellowstone National Park, where my mother was greatly concerned about how many other people had used the blankets we were given. I remember being shown through Paul Revere's house in Boston and being told that he was so stingy that he charged his children rent. I remember stopping in Las Vegas when there were only three or four hotels on the Strip. I remember sitting in a grandstand in a little town in Colorado where a man who owned Arabian stallions put on a Sunday morning horse show that included riders in Arab costumes. I remember being shown through the Del Monte canning plant in California; the tour was apparently a courtesy extended to visiting grocers. I remember riding through the desert in a car equipped with an early air-cooling device—a canvas bag that was attached in some way to the passenger-side window and succeeded mainly in sloshing water all over my mother whenever my father touched the brakes.

On these trips, my father, a man who during the rest of the year couldn't bear to delegate even the task of getting up at four in the morning to buy produce, went for weeks without calling Kansas City to check on the stores. He was on vacation. My mother often mentioned this capacity for shutting out the business he ordinarily watched over with such care as another example of his will, or his stubbornness. My father had a splendid voice, and he often sang as he drove—songs like "On the Road to Mandalay" and a Russian weeper called "Otchi Tchornyia." When we were in the Southwest, he would keep himself supplied with piñon nuts for sustenance between songs. He'd pop half a handful of them at a time into his mouth—shelling them with his teeth, steadily spitting out bits of shell, and periodically announcing, with some ceremony, that he'd stored a large enough supply of the tiny things in his cheek to have a serious taste. It was a skill I found fully as astonishing as his ability to add as fast as his eye could take in the column of figures.

Occasionally he would point out some sight—maybe a butte, maybe a Burma-Shave sign. My capacity to take in the splendors visible from the car was hampered, of course, by the concentration required to defend half of the backseat from Sukey's incursions, the imaginary line down the seat having created a situation that I later compared to the border tension between Finland and the Soviet Union. In this comparison I thought of myself as Finland. At one point, probably after what foreign correspondents might describe as a skirmish along the disputed border, my father handed down a ruling that fairly reflected his traditionalist views on how males and females should interact but was deeply damaging to my side. "We do not hit girls," he said. "You will never hit Sukey again." Sukey, of course, was not visited with a similar injunction, and I became what amounted to a unilaterally disarmed Finland.

When I wasn't on full border-alert, I spent a lot of time begging my father to stop at one of those roadside zoos on Highway 66 which advertised attractions like albino raccoons. When he finally did, the proprietor ended our tour by demonstrating a game that he said the Indians (or could it have been the cowboys?) played on Saturday nights—a game that was based on ten or twelve dice rolled out of a cup. The last couple of dice seemed to have barely stopped tumbling before he had called out the total and scooped everything back in the cup. In the demonstration, my father won small sums two or three times in a row. There was an opportunity to put his winnings toward a bet that sounded safe and potentially extremely profitable, but my father declined. I was outraged. "You were *winning*!" I kept saying as we climbed back in the car. My father drove on for a while, and then he said, "I wasn't winning." He had known that the preliminary wins were a come-on because, unlike just about everyone else who might stop at the roadside zoo, he could actually add up the dice faster than the man could scoop them back into the cup.

We covered the miles in great gulps of driving; as an American driver, my father was always interested in how many miles we had traveled each day. In that pre–Holiday Inn era, where we stopped was partly a matter of where we found a decent place to spend the night. We had a route —the thick black line—but no reservations. My mother was always the one who got out of the car to have a look at the accommodations being offered. Once, fairly early on in those trips, she returned from some tourist court, shook her head as she got back in the car, and said, "Old and frankish." I have no idea how my mother arrived at the idea that "frankish" meant drab or old-fashioned. My dictionary says that "Frankish" refers to Franks and that a Frank is "a member of one of the Germanic tribes of the Rhine region in the early Christian era, especially one of the Salian Franks who conquered Gaul about A.D. 500 and established an extensive empire." Nothing about decor. But we knew what she had in mind. My father reduced the phrase to initials, a habit of his. For years, whenever my mother returned from an inspection trip shaking her head, he would ask, "O. and F.?"

"O. and F.," my mother would confirm, and we would drive on.

When we headed west, the place we stopped for a while before following another black line back to Kansas City was Los Angeles. We would stay two or three weeks in Santa Monica, in one of those tourist courts which had a U of apartments around a grassy area planted with palm trees and lawn chairs. We spent a lot of time on the beach, where the waves were astonishing to someone used to the water lapping up at the muddy edges of Lake Lotawana. We would usually manage to get into a studio to see some filming— one of my mother's cousins was married to a klieg-light operator—and we would sometimes be in the live audience watching a radio show. Occasionally we'd cruise by movie-star hangouts like the Brown Derby to give Sukey an opportunity to scout for autograph prospects. The California stays would have qualified as American family vacations without care, I suppose, except that my father talked a lot about moving to California permanently.

From earliest childhood on, I heard moving to California discussed around our house. I think my father must have been hooked during that first trip we took before the war. Although Bob Hope was already making jokes about smog and freeway traffic, California was not yet California. It was Oregon. That is, in the fantasies of a lot of Midwesterners, it was the clean, beautiful place of fresh weather and fresh starts—the place where people put behind them the harsh winters and the harsh realities of life in the middle of the country. The talk about moving must have been suspended from the time I was around six to the time I was around ten; people didn't move anywhere during the war unless they had to. After the war, it started again. It must have seemed more serious when my father began selling his grocery stores.

My mother and father didn't argue about moving to California—I never heard them argue about anything—but it was obvious to me that my mother didn't want to go. On those trips, Sukey and I might have had our differences on who was on whose side of the backseat, but we were united on this issue. We didn't want to move to California. I didn't fully comprehend our absolute opposition until I had two children of my own: children are the most conservative of God's creatures. They're loath to surrender the familiar. They have no reason to believe that what they have—what they're reasonably sure they have a firm grasp on—can be replaced. They don't have any experience of cycles—observing things change and then change back—so they tend to think of change as permanent and scary. I liked the school I went to, but even if I hadn't I think the idea of changing to a new school would have horrified me. I liked my house. I liked my neighborhood; I knew my way around it on my bike. I liked the beach in Santa Monica, too, but there wasn't a beach in the world that could make me eager to abandon my hometown.

Sometimes my father would simply admire a town, and talk about what a nice place it would be to live in. Santa

Clara was a town he liked, and so was San Jose—a San Jose of the forties, unrelated to the metropolis of today. Once, in Los Angeles, he went to look at a business—a restaurant downtown. Then we all went there to eat. I remember it as being on the ground floor or maybe even below the ground—a huge, noisy place with a name like Sam's or Jack's or Ed's. This was the moment my father must have been closest to moving to California. What was to keep him in Kansas City? Family. Roots. My mother. Sukey and I. When I was a child, I took the possibility of moving to California as a serious threat, particularly after we went to that restaurant in downtown Los Angeles. Looking back, I'm not sure that my father ever thought he was going to get away with it. My mother was an only child who spoke to her mother every single morning on the telephone until the day my grandmother died. (When Sukey grew up and got married, my mother also spoke to *her* every single morning on the telephone.) My father had family responsibilities himself. My parents' friends and their relatives—two groups with a large overlap—were all in Missouri. I don't think, looking back on it, that there was much of a chance we would have moved to Santa Clara or San Jose or Los Angeles.

Over the years since then, I've sometimes wondered what would have happened if we *had* picked up and moved to California. For some reason, I always took it for granted that we would have had more money. I suppose I assumed that my father's enthusiasm for what was going to happen to a place like San Jose would have been translated into real estate, although there have been enthusiastic people in places like San Jose who have lost their shirts. I doubt if my father would ever have struck it truly rich. He did admire industriousness and ambition—it was a compliment when he called someone a "real go-getter"—but I don't think he had the instincts of an entrepreneur. I remember being with him when he read the obituary of some pioneer of the shaving industry who had accumulated an enormous fortune. My father's response was not awe at the money that imagination and business acumen could bring someone in America but satisfaction in being presented with confirmation of his longtime view that razor blades were seriously overpriced. We weren't going to find out whether California could make a difference in his outlook. As Sukey and I settled into Southwest High School, it gradually became apparent that we were going to stay in Kansas City. I was greatly relieved. It occurs to me now that at around the same time I was counting my blessings my father must have resigned himself to having missed his opportunity.

"This was the moment my father must have been closest to moving to California."

Chapter Eight

He was shrewd about Yale. Taking it for granted that your son was going to do something and having him do it, my father had discovered, were not the same thing. As it turned out, I hadn't been interested in playing the cornet or in becoming a connoisseur of marching-band music or in reading those heroic books he had liked as a boy—books with names like *Right End Emerson*. I always knew that he expected me to go to Yale, but after I reached a certain age he didn't push it. He was quiet when, at the age of thirteen or fourteen, I talked about going to the University of Missouri with my high-school pals. On our trip to the East Coast, he did drive through New Haven so that I could see the campus, but he didn't seem exercised when I sat in the backseat of the car staring at the floor. ("A real Trilinsky," my mother said of my performance on that occasion. "A mule.") When I finally decided, around the last couple of years in high school, that it might be interesting to go to college in the East, he didn't become overly enthusiastic. For a while, in fact, I thought he might be reconsidering his single-minded devotion to Yale. From someone manning the Princeton booth at the college night my high school held every year—it was our third or maybe even fourth annual visit—my father learned that Princeton did not permit undergraduates to have automobiles. That impressed him. I took his sudden interest in Princeton as genuine—my father was, after all, a man who could be mightily impressed by an outright ban—but I suppose it could have been simply a feint, of the sort we rarely saw pulled off successfully at the Golden Gloves.

In the past I've speculated that he named me Calvin because he believed, incorrectly, that it would be an appropriate name for someone at Yale. The specific circumstances of my naming were among the many subjects we never got around to discussing. It might have been that he was simply dressing up the name on my birth certificate the way he later dressed up the official name on the pedigree papers of our bulldog, Buck. My official name was used no more than Buck's was. My parents were willing to name me Calvin, but not to call me Calvin; I was known as Buddy from the start. Sukey had also been given what my parents must have thought of as a fancy name, Elaine Sue, and it, too, was as rarely used as our dining room. Among European Jews it's traditional to name a child in memory of someone. People like my parents tended to fulfill that obligation loosely by giving the child the same Hebrew name as the person being memorialized and an English name that had the same first sound. Like my cousin Keith and my cousin Kenneth, I was named in memory of my father's father—whose own name eventually acquired a consistent spelling of Kusel but was never translated into English. Honoring some other departed relative, my father came up with the rather tony middle name of Marshall. ("It's an old family name," I've sometimes explained. "Not our family, but still an old family name.") I'm sure nobody saw any connection between my first name and John Calvin, the founder of Presbyterianism; I didn't hear of John Calvin until I got to college. It may have been that my father simply saw Calvin as a name that would set me out of the crowd —a yellow tie of a name—but I've always suspected that when he chose my name he could imagine the day that I arrived on the Yale campus and introduced myself to Dink Stover and his mates as Calvin Marshall Trillin. And what if they introduced themselves, in the Stover-era tradition, with names like Mutt and Pudge and Biff? No problem. I'd say, "Just call me Bud."

Like a lot of decisions my father made, the decision about where I was going to go to college—made, I suppose, years before, when it became clear that he himself was not going to be able to go to college—was simple and direct. When I first met Alice, she hadn't been quite sure that I meant to be taken literally about the role that Dink Stover had played in my life, but when she met my father and asked him how I happened to go to Yale all the way from Kansas City, his reply began, "I read this book . . ." *Stover at Yale* was published in 1911 and read by my father as a teenager maybe ten years later. I didn't read the book myself until more than thirty years after I left Yale. A classmate of mine named Roger Dennis Hansen—someone his friends had talked about as a man who might one day be the President of the United States, someone my father had met during commencement weekend and then often asked after—committed suicide in 1991. Shortly after the memorial service, I began working on a book called *Remembering Denny*, which somehow became imbued with memories of my father. Reading *Stover* at last, I found that Dink had values that coincided with, or maybe helped form, the values I associated with my father—particularly the values that had to do with upright behavior.

Long after I got out of college, I learned that my father's early exposure to *Stover* had inspired him to start a Yale fund for me when he was still in that first tiny grocery store, before I was born: he put aside the rebate that one of the bread companies offered for prominent display and quick payment. My father's Grand Plan, I think, began with my going to Yale—not on a shoestring, but in the way the sons of the industrialists went to Yale. I would then be not simply a real American, unencumbered by poverty and Old World views, but a privileged American—an American whose degree could give him a place on some special, reservations-only escalator to success. After that, it was up to me. The family joke was that he expected me to be the President of the United States; in reality, I think, he simply expected something out of the ordinary. "It was a first-generation American dream of surpassing corniness," I wrote in *Remembering Denny*, "and I don't think it ever occurred to my father that it might not work out."

But what if it hadn't? What if, for instance, I had been dyslexic? What if it had become obvious at some point that I wasn't capable of making the sort of high-school grades necessary to get into Yale, even in that more accepting era? What if I had been pathologically shy instead of merely as incapable of bringing up awkward subjects as my father was? Would he have dropped the Grand Plan? Parents routinely grope around for the line between encouragement and pressure. He seemed to sense where it was. He was never the sort of parent who demanded to know why the B in some course wasn't an A. I was simply aware that my performance at school wasn't expected to be "ordinary"—a term he used for whatever struck him as not up to the mark, whether it was a meal or a movie or a report card. (One step below that was "*very* ordinary.") Years after I was out of college, I learned that the Yale movie playing in his mind had originally included some footage of me performing as a running back in the Stover mold. I took the absence of such scenes in the version I'd known about as an indication that my father had been capable of making some quiet adaptations in the Grand Plan if there were signs that it was unrealistic in its pure form.

Except for that last-minute feint toward Princeton, he seemed unwavering in his assumption that I would go to Yale. When I was in about the eighth grade, the public-school year in Kansas City ended in April, because of lack of funds. Until it became certain that the financial problems were going to be solved, he held out the threat of sending me to the local private school for boys; Yale obviously did not accept students from non-accredited school systems.

(The private school was called Pembroke Country Day, or Pem-Day, and we called its students "pemsy daisies." I told my father that I would never cross its threshold—although I had, of course, said something similar about the Boy Scouts.) In my senior year in high school, I was offered a Navy ROTC scholarship, but not to Yale: I had been assigned to the University of Missouri. Unlike Yale scholarships, which were not given to people who could pay the tuition, whether their resources sprang from a trust fund or from a bread rebate, this one was not based on need. Although I had no idea what our resources were, I assumed that paying for me to go to Yale was not a trivial matter. I went to my father—he was reading the newspaper in the living room—and told him that I'd be happy to go to the University of Missouri. That was true. It really didn't make much difference to me. He didn't say a word. He just waved me out of the room.

The Yale alumnus who was assigned to interview me was, by chance, a member of the family that had employed my family in the cabinetmaking factory in St. Joe—a coincidence that apparently didn't strike my father as any sort of big deal, since I didn't learn of it until years later. The alumnus who manned the Yale booth at Southwest college nights was not long out of Yale himself; he was from an established Kansas City family, and he'd been to boarding school in the East. At our final college night, my father asked him two questions that astonished me. One was whether Yale had any sort of business training, since, he said, he wouldn't want me to come out of college not even knowing rudimentary bookkeeping. I wasn't astonished at the juxtaposition of bookkeeping and Yale; for all I knew, accounting could have been a popular major there. I was astonished because one of the messages I had taken from my upbringing was that I wasn't going to have to be involved with business. Actually, I had gotten the impression that I was expected to be above such matters as perusing the business pages and discussing investments—an impression that I have never exactly abandoned, much to the detriment of my finances. The other question was even more surprising to me. My father asked if Yale had any sort of Jewish quota that could keep me out even if I qualified in every other way. (The representative said that he knew of no such quota. A decade later, it was revealed, to my great surprise, that the percentage of Jews in Yale College was not only the lowest in the Ivy League but also suspiciously consistent from year to year.) Although I had heard of quotas, which I associated with medical schools, I had never heard my father bring up the subject. I had never heard him acknowledge any limitations on what was available to me.

Looking back, I think that with the first step of the Grand Plan—my application to Yale—close at hand, he may have had just a moment of doubt. Was this really going to happen? If it did, was it really the right thing for me? The next moment, the doubt was gone. It came back, I think, several years later. As I was finishing Yale, I was sort of becalmed. I had no idea of what I wanted to do, and I had no immediate plans to do anything. My father decided that I should go to law school and think about coming back to Kansas City to work with some lawyers he knew. In *Remembering Denny*, I reported what I finally said to him: "You used to think I was going to be President. Now you think I should come back and advise somebody on the tax implications of his real estate deal? This is quite a comedown."

In between those two moments of doubt, it didn't seem to surprise my father that Yale worked out for me pretty much the way he had expected it to. As it turned out, he had also understood the drawbacks in the way it was likely to work out for him and my mother. When I got on the train to New Haven, in the autumn of 1953, I assumed that after four years I would be coming back home; in choosing among the sports available in the exercise program required of Yale freshmen then, I remember deciding that squash made no sense for me, since I didn't know of any squash court closer to Kansas City than St. Louis, 250 miles away. But I know now that my father had resigned himself from the start to the probability that a Yale education would put a distance between me and my family forever—a cultural distance and probably even a geographical distance. I know because many years later my mother told me so, making it clear from her tone that sending me to Yale had not been her decision and that, to some extent, she'd always resented it. Thinking back to the conversations among adults I heard in those days, it occurs to me that my father's dream of his son at Yale ran counter to the conventional wisdom about college among the people he knew—almost all of whom were also first-generation Americans who hadn't been to college themselves. They thought it was sensible to go to somewhere like the University of Missouri because they saw college partly as a place where a young man gets to know the people he'll live among and do business with for the rest of his life. It was not an argument that would have had any impact on my father. He didn't expect me to be living among the people who went to the University of Missouri. He didn't expect me to be doing business with anybody.

When I was home during a Yale break, my father would usually insist on taking me for a clothes-shopping expedition that I look back on as something close to a parody of the cultural tensions in store for a Midwestern family that sent a son to a place as removed from our experience as Yale then was. Even if I had gone to the University of Missouri, shopping for clothes would have presented a problem for us. My father was a strong believer in highly shined shoes and carefully folded pocket handkerchiefs; by his standards, I was only sporadically presentable. The outings were doubly complicated by the fact that what was to be called the Ivy Look had not yet made its way across the country, so the clothes for sale in even the best stores of Kansas City simply didn't look much like what people at Yale wore. Somehow, I couldn't seem to get this across to my father. As we drove home from Wolff Brothers and Jack Henry Men's Clothing, having bagged only a single shirt or a pair of trousers I knew I'd never wear, the silence in the car was less comfortable than the silence had been in those drives to the city market.

My father was still weak from the heart attack when he and my mother came to New Haven for commencement. I remember arranging to pick them up at the railroad station through some special exit so that he wouldn't have to walk up the stairs. On the day before the formal commencement at Yale, there is a ceremony for the graduating seniors called

Class Day, and I was among those delivering speeches. My speech, the Class History, was meant to be funny. It used what passed for cynicism in my circle to talk about how Yale had prepared us for the world. After it was over, my father turned to Denny Hansen, who was sitting next to him, and said cheerfully, "If I thought he believed any of that, I'd have him shot." I don't know if I believed any of it, but by then I knew that my father's view of Yale as a place whose main purpose was to provide a reservation on the magic escalator—what I described in *Remembering Denny* as a place that would "turn the likes of us into the likes of them"—was not my view. A year before, an opportunity to explain that to him had come up with the approach of Tap Day—the event that in those quaint times decided whether a junior would be admitted beyond the Yale College equivalent of the pearly gates. Because I was the editor of the newspaper, I was likely to be tapped by one or another of the senior societies, and if that happened I wasn't certain whether or not I would accept. Not accepting a tap was a notion so contrary to my father's Storesque view of Yale that I thought it required explanation. Sitting in my office at the *Yale Daily News* very late one night, I started a letter to him. I was on the third page when I gave it up. I had decided that it was too late to begin explaining that my view of what I was doing there was not precisely the same as his. Or maybe I was having trouble trying to explain precisely what my view was. Or maybe even I had realized that discussing my reservations about the extracurricular Yale so important to Dink Stover might sound hypocritical in a letter written from an office where

I spent a lot more time every day than I spent at the library. Or maybe I'd decided that it was too late at night to write such a letter. I still think of it as the moment I might have broken the silence that I remember from those long drives to the city market.

As it turned out, I decided to join a society anyway, and called my father after Tap Day to tell him.

"That's not the one Stover was in, is it?" he said.

"No, it's the other one," I said, and wondered if he had been following along with the book the whole time.

I graduated thinking that I was grateful for the aspirations of my father that sent me there, even if I considered it obvious that the effect of the experience on me had been more in the way I thought and what I thought about than in the sort of career opportunities I'd been given. Fifteen years or so later, I happened to attend a birthday dinner that was made up mostly of people in my line of work, all of whom were doing all right and some of whom were pretty well known, as non-fiction writers go. At dinner, there were a couple of tables of ten, and at our table someone brought up the name of somebody whom, we quickly realized, everyone present had met through a different connection. I looked around at my tablemates, and realized that they had all been to the same sort of college that I had been to. That was true of all but a couple of people at the other table, too. Passengers on the magic escalator? Until then, I hadn't thought of writing as a trade that depends much on Ivy League credentials. Unlike, say, being the vice president of a bank or the trust partner of a law firm, it does, after all, require you to reveal your work to the public at

"My father was still weak from the heart attack when he and my mother came to New Haven for commencement."

(IN FRONT, FROM LEFT: ABE TRILLIN, MARSHALL J. DODGE III, ROGER DENNIS HANSEN)

large. Was the fact that we had reached the point of having our writing published by prominent magazines or respectable book publishers strongly connected to the fact we had all gone to the same sort of colleges and universities? I put my own work history into reverse, and realized that it had flowed naturally from a summer job at *Time*. And what had led to the summer job? The *Yale Daily News*. For the first time, I realized that my father's vision of how all of this was supposed to work out might not have been as simplistic as I had always assumed. "My God!" I said to Alice on the way home that night. "Could he have been right?"

Chapter Nine

If my father started reading a book, he finished
it, whether he liked it or not. He read all sorts
of books. He read good books and he read trash.
He finished them all. I tried to persuade him that
giving up on a book is not a reflection of weak
character but simply a decision to spend your
reading time elsewhere; as my mother would
have said, it was like talking to the wall. At times,
he'd say something that sounded as if it might
have been designed to get a rise out of me or
Uncle Jerry, the librarian. "I don't understand
what they see in this Faulkner," he said once,
when I was in college—which might have drawn
an erudite response from me if I hadn't been
having so much trouble getting through *Absalom, Absalom!* He was strongly in favor of plot.
There wasn't any question about who his favorite
writer was—O. Henry. He liked short stories with
those little reverse flips at the end—just the sort

of thing that the instructors in the writing course at Yale told us not to think of turning in.

When I was a child, we didn't have a lot of books around. We lived in the same house—the house my father had built in the Country Club District just as the war was about to start—from the time I was five to the time Sukey got married, when I was halfway through college. Going over the rooms in my mind now, I can't picture any bookcases, except for a couple of shelves in a finished basement that we referred to as the recreation room (I can picture *Right End Emerson* on those shelves). In fact, my father sometimes said that he didn't understand why Uncle Jerry, who was raising a family on the salary of a city librarian, had so many books in the house. It wasn't as if a librarian had any problem of access to books he might want to read, and at no cost. What was the point of buying a lot of books and keeping them even after you'd read them? He wasn't exactly being critical of Uncle Jerry. He used the phrase he'd use if I remarked, say, that going to Europe for a while after college might be the sort of thing I'd like to do: "What's the advantage?" He didn't mean the word "advantage" in the sense of taking advantage or gaining some advantage; he used it to question whether something that seemed frivolous or luxurious was truly necessary and sensible. My father had a strong sense of enoughness.

In his late fifties, years after those discussions about Uncle Jerry's books, he started buying books himself. I think it came about because garage sales became a custom in Kansas City. Once, when I was home visiting, he took me out to his car to show me what he had acquired that afternoon.

He opened the trunk of the old Thunderbird he had then. It was full of books.

"A dollar," he said.

"A dollar a book?" I said.

He shook his head. "A dollar," he said.

Someone he knew who was closing down a shoe store had some shelves on his hands, and my father put them in the basement to use for the books he bought. After a while, I got him a subscription to a newsletter that carries ads from people who are looking for hard-to-find books. He sold some of the books through the ads, and he spent a lot of time arranging them in proper categories, and, of course, he would often read one—all the way to the end. He himself became surrounded by books, but he didn't become a collector, the way my Uncle Jerry is a collector. His main source for buying books remained garage sales. He once said to me, "I never pay more than a dime for a book unless it's something special."

I don't think I'd had any inkling that my father did any writing himself until around the time I was in high school, when rhyming couplets began to appear daily on the lunch menu at Trillin's restaurant. When it became known that my father had bought Hoover's, the question I was most asked about it was whether he had any plans to change the chef. The answer to that was no; the chef, the only black man I ever met named Otto, remained. The sort of food Otto prepared didn't change much; the dinner menu still featured items like roast turkey with stuffing and prime ribs of beef au jus. What did change was the lunch menu, which my father, who had learned typing at Robidoux Polytechnic

High School, typed up every day. A lot of the lunchtime customers were regulars—salesmen who called routinely in the area, merchants from small shopping centers in what was essentially a residential district—and many of them sat at the counter so that they could spend part of their lunch hour passing the time with my father. The lunch menu also reflected more or less the same food that had always been served at Hoover's in the middle of the day, but its way of describing the food changed. Sometimes, for instance, there was something called Turkey Tetrazzini on the menu—I suspect that had some connection with how much roast turkey was sold the previous evening—and my father always announced it with the phrase "Try Trillin's Terrific Turkey Tetrazzini." Fairly soon after he took over the restaurant, he began including couplets on the lunch menu, most of them about pie.

I discussed the couplets in the first book I did about eating, *American Fried*: "When it came to poetry, my father was not an absolutist. Pie was his favorite subject for a couplet, but every three or four weeks he would write about something else—perhaps a couplet like ' "Eat your food," gently said Mom to little son Roddy / "If you don't, I will break every bone in your body." ' The next day he would be back to pies—'Mrs. Trillin's pecan pie, so nutritious and delicious / Will make a wild man mild and a mild man vicious' or 'A woman shot her husband in our place last July / He started talking while she was enjoying her pie.' He made a strong case in the poems for the pies being completely free of calories. 'Don't blame your weight / On the pie you ate,' he would write, or 'So you love the sound of the soft-lowing cattle / Then eat lots of pie and be lighter in the saddle.' He often returned to the theme of pie being good for one's general health, like mineral water or brisk walks. 'A piece of pie baked by Mrs. Trillin,' he would write of a pie baked, of course, by a black woman named Thelma, 'will do you more good than penicillin.' He rhymed pie with 'eye' and 'goodbye' and 'fry' (' "Let's go, warden, I'm ready to fry / My last request was Mrs. Trillin's pie" ') and 'evening is nigh.' His shortest poem, as far as I can tell, was 'Don't sigh / Eat pie.' "

When he was more or less semiretired, he wrote down a number of anecdotes. He typed them, each on a separate piece of almost square white paper. They were all typed with no strikeovers, and, as I recall, they all took up precisely the full page. My father strongly believed that neatness counts. He once caught a glimpse of a manuscript of mine—neat by my standards, which is to say that it was perfectly legible, with corrections done by blacking out the replaced word and typing the new word above it. He responded the way he'd responded in my high-school days whenever he noticed my footwear, which almost never showed signs of having put in any time at the shoe-shining apparatus he kept in the basement. I now can't find my father's neatly typed anecdotes, although Sukey came across the list of topics he was presumably working from. It also is neat—sixty-four topics, listed down the page in block letters and numbered.

Very few of them conjure up stories I can remember hearing him tell. They do confirm my recollection that many of the stories he liked were about life in the grocery

business—"My first holdup" and "The ice machine episode" and "The Heinz soup deal" and "The shooting of the
milk man" and "The night Edyth was held up" and "My
second holdup—locked in ice box." Some of them—"Miss
Wiehl and the whipping at Eugene Field" and "The first
Armistice Day—the lost cap" and, of course, "Jesse James
barn and my dislocated shoulder"—concerned memories
my father had of his childhood in St. Joe. One of those, I
suspect, sounds racier than the story that went with it—
"The episode of Red Agron and the married blond." Red
Agron was a childhood friend of my father's in St. Joe, and
I remember my father's telling stories about him that por-
trayed him as an entertaining scamp, a sort of Jewish Tom
Sawyer. Decades after they'd lost track of each other, they
met by chance in Mexico, and my father reported that Red
Agron hadn't changed much. If a peddler making the rounds
of tables on the square at Cuernavaca was selling a rug for,
say, seventy-four pesos, Red Agron's first move was to offer
him eight.

A lot of topics on the list—"Little J.B. and the rat in the
tub of spinach," say, or "Jonesy and the red pepper in the
cookies" or "Joe Starr and the laxative tablets"—reflected
my father's fascination with life imitating practical jokes.
There were ten items on the list involving automobiles—
buying them, selling them, running them into buildings.
A lot of the stories were about misadventure. Both Sukey's
birth and my birth made the list that way. Number 14 is
"Sukey's birth—drove past hospital." Number 16 is "Buddy's birth—key lost."

After my mother died, I found pieces of my father's writing I hadn't known about, most of them written before I was born. There were several pieces, some of them in the form of letters to my mother before my parents were married, that were done in hillbilly dialect. There were three stories. One of them was about a widow in a Russian village near Kiev called Sikeelcha, which has been raided by a murderous band of irregulars. Despite a horsewhipping ordered by the raiders' pitiless Cossack leader, the widow refuses to divulge the hiding place of the money she has hidden away for the support of her child. The raiders are called away before they have time to finish beating the widow to death—and then it turns out that, because a new government has changed the currency, the money that the widow protected is worthless. The other stories also had the sort of switcheroo endings that O. Henry favored. One of them, written in Yiddish, was about a hobo who commits a lot of crimes in the hope of being arrested and given a warm bed in jail. The other was a thirty-eight-page comic short story about a large young black woman in Georgia trying to do away with her smaller and much older husband; its dialogue was in a broad version of a Southern black dialect. A thirty-eight-page short story is a serious effort. The pieces made me wonder if my father ever harbored ambitions to be a writer—not someone who wrote down anecdotes as a way to pass the time in retirement but a *writer*.

My parents used to tell a story of the sort all parents tell about the cute comments their kids have made: my father said to me, when I was three or four, that a newspaperman might be an interesting thing for me to be and I replied, "Okay, Daddy, if you want me to sell newspapers, I'll sell newspapers." It was years after I had heard that devastatingly amusing punch line a few hundred times that I began to wonder about the straight line that had set it up. Was a newspaperman what he wanted me to be? Did sending me to typing school have anything to do with that? The year the Kansas City public-school classes ended in April, my father sent Sukey and me to a place called Sarachon-Hooley Secretarial School to learn how to type—partly, I think, on the theory that typing was a useful skill and partly in the belief that kids should not be wandering free in April. After the course, Sukey was liberated for the summer, but I was made to type forty-five minutes a day—the opposite of what you'd expect in an era when typing was considered good training for girls. But would that be how you'd steer your son toward journalism—slip the word to him casually when he's three years old and then make sure he knows how to type?

"'I don't understand what they see in this Faulkner,' he said once, when I was in college—which might have drawn an erudite response from me if I hadn't been having so much trouble getting through 'Absalom, Absalom!'"

Chapter Ten

I once did an article on the fiftieth anniversary of something called the Coops, a cooperative apartment complex in the Bronx founded by Jewish garment workers whose politics were reflected in the fact that they had a youth club named after one of the Scottsboro boys and another youth club called Teivos, Soviet spelled backward. In the twenties, I discovered, a Jewish garment worker would have thought nothing of choosing an apartment building according to his political beliefs. A follower of the Social Democratic wing of the Jewish labor movement, for instance, would have avoided the Coops and applied to a similar building sponsored by the Amalgamated Clothing Workers. In fact, when Jay Lovestone and his followers were expelled from the American Communist Party, Lovestonites disappeared from the board of directors of the Coops, not to be trusted even with decisions on electrical wiring and plumbing repairs ("Their politics naturally influenced their general thinking," I was told by one of the original residents). At some point in the research, it dawned on me that the people I was interviewing—people who had lived in a world that seemed exotic to me—had come from Eastern Europe at about the same time my family came, and from the same sorts of places. I can't imagine that when the Coops opened in 1929, any of my relatives in Missouri had ever heard of Jay Lovestone. I suspect many of them might have had trouble placing Trotsky.

New York also had plenty of nonpolitical Jewish immigrants, of course, but it occurred to me that the differences in outlook that separated my relatives from the early Coops residents came largely from the geographical vagaries of an emigration that had deposited the Trilinskys in a place where people talked a lot about agriculture and not at all about the Schachtmanite deviation. I suppose a certain number of Jews leaving Eastern Europe did choose their destinations for reasons that reflected the sort of people they were. Those who were radicals in the old country must have gravitated to New York; the Coops had a group of residents called nineteen-fivers, for instance, who couldn't trouble themselves with American politics because they were deeply immersed in arguing about what went wrong in the Russian Revolution of 1905. But for the great mass of Jews eager to leave Eastern Europe in those days, it seems to me, which culture the next generation would be raised in was decided by the luck of the boat. Our boat went to Galveston, and I was raised by a man whose "general thinking" was, to a great extent, Midwestern.

Kansas City had poor Jews, but it had no Jewish proletariat. (When my mother returned from a trip to New York, she always said, "In New York, Jews do everything"—reflecting her astonishment once again at encountering Jewish policemen and cabdrivers and waiters.) We didn't know any left-wingers; we didn't know that the right-wingers we knew were right-wingers. My mother referred to a man one of her cousins had married as a Bolshevik, but I think that meant he came from people who didn't go to the synagogue even on Yom Kippur. In the Kansas City of my childhood, politics meant Democrat or Republican—and in my family not even much of that. I'm sure my parents voted for Roosevelt, but I think that they also voted for Eisenhower. A lot of people in Kansas City of my father's generation thought of Harry Truman as a Pendergast machine pol who wasn't really up to the job. My father may have voted for Truman, but he didn't identify with him. (After the fact, that struck me as odd, because reading David McCullough's biography of Truman made me think of my father constantly—the optimism, the faith in the work ethic, the blunt honesty, the confidence that neatness counts.) I can remember my father's repeating strong opinions about, say, movies ("I don't care what you say. *Gunga Din* is the best movie ever made") or food ("There's nothing better than a fresh ear of corn"), but not about politics.

The St. Joseph of my father's childhood was more heterogeneous than the association with the Pony Express might suggest. It had a concentration of meat-packing houses that required a supply of people willing to do unpleasant work cheaply—Polish immigrants, for instance, and more black people than might be expected in a small city that far north. My father had grown up next door to a black family without thinking much of it, and he often said so. He seemed to have only one group prejudice, but it was a beaut: he didn't like refugees. I suppose a certain number of Jews who were escaping Hitler came to Kansas City before the war, and I think a program that saw some significance in involving Harry Truman's hometown brought quite a few Holocaust survivors just after the war. My father, as he would have put it, wasn't crazy about them. Like most prejudices, his antipathy toward refugees was not easily explained, but at the center of it, I think, was a feeling that the refugees he came across were simply not becoming Americanized at a pace commensurate with what they owed this country and what made good sense. Once, when we were talking about one of his hospital stays, the subject of his roommate came up, and he shook his head. "Refugees," he said.

When I reminded him that he himself could be described as a refugee, he told me that when people visited the roommate they spoke only in German.

"But if your mother had been in the hospital and you went to visit her, you'd have spoken to her in Yiddish," I said.

"I don't care what you say," he said. "They should speak English. This is America."

My father practiced what people schooled in intellectual

discourse call reductionism. He often said something to which it was possible to respond, "Well, it's really more complicated than that." Sometimes it was more complicated than that, and sometimes it wasn't. His opinion about the relative merits of movies and the theater was an example of his tendency to boil things down. Movies were better than plays, he always said, because when the action of a movie took place on the top of a mountain you were actually on the top of a mountain. I had a notion that it was really more complicated than that, but I was never absolutely certain in just which way. In the early sixties, my parents visited me while I was working in the Atlanta bureau of *Time*, covering the civil rights struggle, and we all had a drink at the home of a college friend's parents—people who thought of themselves as relatively enlightened Southerners. During a lull in the conversation, my father said, "I never understood what you people in the South had against colored people." There was some scrambling among the rest of us, including me, to explain how complicated it all was.

Religion was fairly easy to boil down. He had grown up in an Orthodox Jewish family. His mother, who moved to Kansas City some time during my childhood, remained what some people would call an observant Jew and what my mother preferred to call "a religious fanatic." Although we had food specially prepared for my father's mother when she came to our house so that she wouldn't have to eat anything that wasn't kosher, she never ate any of it. She felt about the food in our house more or less the way my mother felt about the other Cub Scouts' meat loaf. Given parents of that sort, my father must have spent a lot of his childhood in a synagogue rather than on the roof of Jesse James's barn. He could do the sort of Hebrew chanting that's so fast the words run together; whenever I thought about how many hours of Hebrew instruction must have gone into creating that sort of speed, I shuddered. His stint in Hebrew school had not instilled a great reverence for Talmudic study; if someone mentioned a distinguished fore-bear in the Old Country who had devoted his life to schol-arship, my father was likely to nod his head and say, "Couldn't make a living." What he had figured out about Jewish prayer, he often said, was that no matter how long the service lasted, there were basically five things said. I can't remember what they were, but I assume one of them was that God is sovereign and another was that He is the only God and another was that the worshippers are grateful to Him. Whatever those five points were, my father figured that no purpose was served by repeating them again and again. Was God hard of hearing? As a boy, my father re-solved that when he grew up he'd go to the synagogue whose service started latest and got out the earliest. There would still be plenty of time for the five points to be made—maybe even two or three times, but not all day.

He meant that in a limited way. There was never any chance, I think, of my father's going to the Reform temple, which at that time conducted virtually its entire service in English and didn't even have bar mitzvahs. There was never any chance of his not going to the synagogue every day for a year to say Kaddish after his mother died. There was never any chance that I wouldn't have a bar mitzvah or that we would not celebrate Passover with my mother's parents.

(The few sips of wine required to say the blessings made my father so sleepy that my mother always had to drive home.) He paid his dues to the Conservative synagogue. He gave his contribution to the United Jewish Appeal. On Rosh Hashanah and Yom Kippur, he went to the synagogue, even though he knew that a long time would be taken for the five points to be made.

In fact, the eve of Rosh Hashanah was one of our ritual outings: my father and I always attended services with Pop at his synagogue while the women remained at my grandparents' to prepare the meal. My grandparents did not belong to the main Orthodox synagogue; they belonged to a small congregation that was always referred to around our house as Coxey's Army—presumably after the ragtag army of unemployed that Jacob Coxey led to Washington in 1894. (Years later, working on a story in the South, I came across a similar congregation, composed of mainly older people, and it was also known as Coxey's Army.) The Kansas City version of Coxey's Army seemed to me as chaotic as the original. The officers of the congregation sat on a stage in the front of the room, but the service was conducted from a platform somewhere in the middle. Women were in the balcony. There was an enormous din at all times—people talking, children running up and down the aisles, old men shouting that whoever was leading the services had skipped something important. When the din became unbearable, the president of the synagogue would rise from his seat on the stage, walk to a podium, slam his hand down, and shout, *"Shveig! Shveig!"* The noise would subside for a

couple of minutes, and then gradually return to the roar
that had brought the president to the podium in the first
place.

In a way, the service on the eve of Rosh Hashanah was
opening night: Coxey's Army was not large enough to em-
ploy a regular *chazzen*, or cantor, so someone was hired
just for the High Holy Days of Rosh Hashanah and Yom
Kippur. I assume that this person came from New York,
the Capital of the Jews; there were obviously no spare cantors
in Topeka or Sedalia. Every year, as we left Coxey's Army,
my father and Pop had the same conversation about the
cantor.

"That was the worst *chazzen* I've ever heard," my father
would say. "He sounds like he's in pain. I don't see how
you're going to make it to Yom Kippur, Pop."

Pop never seemed to hear that remark. Just after my father
spoke, Pop would say, "The *chazzen*'s not too bad this year.
Not too bad."

After the minimum of observance had been satisfied—
after my father had done what it would have been disre-
spectful to his upbringing not to do—he was uninvolved in
organized religion. He never went to the synagogue except
on the High Holy Days. He had no interest in being, say,
an officer of the synagogue, which he saw in some cases as
an opportunity to strut on the stage during Rosh Hashanah
and Yom Kippur. In our house, an officer of the synogogue,
particularly one who seemed to make more of a production
of his public role than was called for, ran the risk of being
referred to as a big *k'nocker*. After I left home, my father

never asked about whether I went to the synagogue. Unlike my mother, he seemed to have no interest in whether or not I married someone who was Jewish.

When my parents met Alice, while they were on a visit to New York, it was the first time they had been introduced to someone they had reason to believe I might, as my mother would have put it, bring home. They were noncommittal when, on the way in from the airport, I finally produced Alice's last name; it was Stewart. I did not mention that her mother was Jewish—not then and not even after we were well into dinner in Chinatown that evening with Alice and some other friends. I suppose my refusal to volunteer that information ended any small doubts that might have existed about whether I took after the St. Joe people. Finally, after my mother gamely began a couple of sentences to Alice "In our religion . . . ," Alice realized that some information had been withheld, and supplied it herself. When the phrase "half-Jewish" came up, I said that there was no such thing as half-Jewish, since Jews believe in matrilineal succession: if your mother is Jewish, you're Jewish. A few days after my parents got back to Kansas City, my mother phoned and said, "I happened to be talking to Rabbi Hadas, and he says you're right about that matrilineal succession business."

"Oh, you just happened to run into Rabbi Hadas on the Plaza and you two fell into another one of your Talmudic discussions?"

"Anyway," she said. "He says you're right."

From earliest childhood, I heard my mother say that she would accept anyone I brought home, but it was always clear to me that she dreaded the thought of a non-Jewish daughter-in-law. I don't think that had much to do with concerns about the religious upbringing of her grandchildren. She was no more religious than my father was. It was partly, I believe, that she didn't feel entirely sure of herself socially with Gentiles—a problem my father did not share. He was crazy about Alice from the start, and I think he would have been even if both her parents had turned out to be some variety of the evangelical Christians he always referred to generically as Holy Rollers.

My father took it for granted that I would always be Jewish, whatever the background of the person I married. On the other hand, he didn't exactly raise me to be a Jew; he raised me to be an American. Looking back now at signals I got from him—what he seemed to encourage, what he didn't encourage—I think he would not have been thrilled if I had developed a boyhood passion for, say, Zionism or Orthodox Judaism. Not that either of those was very likely. The first time I ever saw someone walking down the street wearing a yarmulke—let alone side curls—was long after I left Kansas City. I grew up during an era of watered-down religion, before the religious revivals that affected Jews and Gentiles alike in postwar America. Looking back on it, I think I assumed that the real Jews were in New York. In fact, New York was a code word for Jewish in Kansas City, in the way Lincoln was a code word for black—so that blacks went to the movies at the Lincoln and Jews bought bagels at the New York Bakery. New York was also where the real baseball players were—the Kansas City Blues were a farm club of the New York Yankees—and I suppose I saw the situation as somewhat analogous. We were farm-club

Jews. We had some major league people—Gershon Hadas, the rabbi at our synagogue, was a wry and scholarly man whom even I could recognize as extraordinary—but it was basically a farm-club operation. Years later, when I gave a speech at a Jewish community center in the Chicago suburbs, I called it "Midwestern Jews: Making Chopped Liver with Miracle Whip." After the speech, someone came up and said that the title was an interesting metaphor. "It's not a metaphor," I said. "It's a recipe." That was how my mother made chopped liver. I believe she considered schmaltz déclassé.

"When my mother returned from a trip to New York, she always said, 'In New York, Jews do everything'—reflecting her astonishment once again at encountering Jewish policemen and cabdrivers and waiters."

"When my mother first started suggesting that they consider taking a trip to Europe, my father, speaking as someone who had once got his foot stuck in the mud in Russia, always replied, 'I've been.'"

Chapter Eleven

In his late fifties, my father could have been described as semiretired, a man with a damaged heart and reduced energy. I wasn't always given the details of how his health was—on the theory, I think, that someone in New York who was trying to carry the family banner at the same time he was typing with two hands in the prescribed Sarachon-Hooley manner didn't need to be bothered. I went home regularly, but my father and I were still not in the habit of using our time together for heart-to-hearts. What had changed since the days of the silent rides to the city market, I suppose, was that I was aware of what we didn't do. When an offer to move from *Time* to *The New Yorker* came along—through an alignment of circumstances that amounted to a quirk—I phoned him to talk it over, although there had actually never been any doubt in my mind that I was going to take the offer. To my surprise, his enthusiasm was limited—partly, I later realized, because *Time* was a familiar presence in Kansas City and he was barely conscious of *The New Yorker*. He asked me how the salaries compared. There was a long silence on the telephone. Finally, I acknowledged that I hadn't asked about how much I might be making at *The New Yorker*, where writers were basically paid by the piece. He was incredulous. I could picture him sitting at the phone half a continent away, shaking his head slowly at the confirmation of a fear that must have surfaced in his mind more than once—that he had raised a son who was simply not sensible.

The next day, I wrote him a long letter—conscious, I'm sure, of the letter I hadn't sent just before Tap Day at Yale. I discussed in great detail the limitations imposed on writers by the group journalism system then in force at *Time*. I explained that, given the magazine's overriding loyalty to the Republican Party, there would probably come a time when I'd have to leave anyway because of some argument over editing changes—or, worse, not leave because I wanted to avoid the argument. I said that *The New Yorker* would be the ideal forum for all the sorts of writing I wanted to do. I assured him I would explore the question of income, even though in the short run it wouldn't have much impact of my life; I was twenty-seven years old and single and living happily in the Village with no efforts at thrift on a salary of $11,500 a year. The letter was something like thirteen hundred words long. It was carefully constructed. Toward the end of it, I said, "I did want you to know that I'm not just jumping into something, or giving up a good job on a lark." When I wrote the letter, I was under the impression that I was trying to make my father feel included in my decision. Reading it over now, I realize that I was trying to tell him that I was no longer becalmed and that I had caught some of his messages and that I might even be sensible.

After I joined *The New Yorker* and my parents began receiving it by mail, the question my mother asked about the editor was whether or not he was Jewish—presumably on the theory that if he was he might be slightly more reluctant to throw her son out onto the streets in bad times. The question my father asked about the editor was why he didn't display his name somewhere in the magazine. I tried to come up with an answer that sounded knowing—although once I started considering the question, I realized that every other magazine I was familiar with did have a masthead that included the editor's name. "I don't care what you say," said my father, who had, after all, put his own name on both a supermarket and a restaurant, "if I put out a magazine that I was proud of, I'd put my name on it."

In those years, my father went to the office some. My parents continued taking the sort of long automobile trips around the country that had begun when I was a child. When my mother first started suggesting that they consider taking a trip to Europe, my father, speaking as someone who had once got his foot stuck in the mud in Russia, always replied, "I've been." Sooner or later, though, he gave in; it was on the way back from a trip to Europe that they met Alice. On the days when my father wasn't feeling well, Sukey often went over to keep him company. After a couple of years at the University of Colorado, she had indeed returned to Kansas City to marry and produce the requisite grandchildren—three boys. A friend had a farm with a pond on it, and my father spent a lot of time there fishing, sometimes with one of my nephews. He bought trunkloads of books at garage sales. When I saw him, he never spoke of illness, but he was obviously in fragile health.

When the call came, Alice and I had just arrived at a little seaside resort near Malindi, on the coast of Kenya, where we were intending to stay a couple of weeks while I wrote something I had researched in Malawi. Not long after checking in, we had gone into town to pick up some snorkeling equipment. It was August of 1967. My father was sixty years old. I don't think I always had the fragility of his health in mind, but when we returned from our trip to town and were told by the proprietor that there had been a call for me from the United States, the first thing I thought of was that my father was dead.

The funeral is sort of a blur now. I do remember that in the eulogy the rabbi—the successor to Rabbi Hadas—said that when he visited my father in the hospital once and they'd had a talk about the new novel by Chaim Potok, he understood that my father wasn't truly under the impression that the author's name was Chaim Pupik. (In Yiddish, *pupik* means navel, but it's somehow funnier to say "I was up to my *pupik* in Republicans" than "I was up to my navel in Republicans." I suppose something about the *pupik* of a Litvak would be almost automatically funny.) After several days of receiving people at our house, Pop and I started going to the synagogue every evening to say Kaddish. I was there at my mother's request. Mildly resentful at having to perform what seemed to me a public relations function, I viewed my fellow mourners—mostly men nearer my father's age—as people honoring their obligations in the most cursory way. My father had referred to the regulars as the Kaddish Club. They were always impatient to start the service precisely at six. As it ended, they were out the door and into their cars, and you could almost hear the golf clubs rattling in the trunks. I may have resented them a bit for being alive; there is, after all, nothing in the Talmud about not playing golf after you say Kaddish.

Then, one evening, Rabbi Hadas, who was living nearby in retirement, appeared in the small congregation. Just before the grumbling to begin got started, he rose from his seat and said, "Well, we have a minute and a half until six, and tomorrow's Tisha b'Av, so I think I'll take the minute and a half to explain Tisha b'Av." It was a classic Rabbi Hadas opening: the allusion to the minute and a half said everything he needed to say about the haste with which the Kaddish Club performed its duties. He said that Tisha b'Av meant the ninth of Av, in the Hebrew calendar—the date of the destruction of the First Temple. After mentioning that the ninth of Av was also thought to be the day the Second Temple was destroyed, he listed a few other catastrophic events that might have taken place on that dismal day, showing less certainty with each event he mentioned. Then he said that the important point was not whether these things had literally happened on this precise date but that observing the ninth of Av as a day of sadness gave us a sense of continuity, which was central to Judaism. Then he said that the reason we were there saying Kaddish was this sense of continuity. Then he sat down. It had taken only a minute and a half.

At some point in the first week after my father died, my mother and I went down to the basement to recover a thick wad of emergency cash that she said my father always kept back in the workings of the central air-conditioning system—presumably the last place the Cossacks would look. A lot of people came to our house in those first days, many of them bearing casseroles or baked goods. They told a lot of stories about him. When I thought I might lose control, I went out in the backyard; my father had not been enthusiastic about men crying in public. People who used to work in the grocery stores came. Some of the waitresses from the restaurant came. The man who had been my father's partner in the subdivision came. He had always struck me as the sort of contractor who had grown up in the country and learned construction putting up fences or repairing barns. Drawing me aside, he told me that when the subdivision was not going well my father could have abandoned him —there had been no contractual obligation to stay—but had chosen not to, at considerable risk. He said that he would never forget it. When the crowds had thinned out, a man who had gotten to know my father at garage sales came by, inspected every book in the basement, presented me with a list of the ones I might want to save or sell because of their value, and eventually arranged to have the rest donated to a new college—a Nazarene college, I think, or maybe Assembly of God—in my father's name. A lot of the men who came to our house during those days came up to me before they left and asked if they could have one of my father's yellow ties to remember him by.

Chapter Twelve

So he had been right about that, too—even the yellow ties. I don't mean that he was right about everything. Some things are, in fact, more complicated than he thought they were, or at least than he said they were. Sometimes, obviously, it's all right to do something—something unnecessary or maybe something not very sensible—even if it would have caused my father to ask, "What's the advantage?" We know now —and some people knew then—that daughters and sons can be raised with similar aspirations. Basically, though, I think I've accepted most of my father's messages, with just a little light editing here and there. Living in New York, whose customs sometimes strike someone from the Middle West as being much more like the Middle East, I eventually learned to deal routinely with people who do not always live up to his black-and-white standards of upright behavior. Still, I have sometimes heard myself say of a shop whose proprietor has done something my father would have considered improper, "I'll never go into that place again"—despite Alice's arguing that what the proprietor did wasn't the worst thing in the world and that he doesn't have a terribly pleasant life and that a permanent boycott seems a bit harsh. But I know I'll never go into that place again, because we are, after all, stubborn people. When my daughters reached the age of twelve, I didn't make a point of insisting that they pay full fare at the movies, but only because it would have made me feel priggish and self-righteous. Not that I haven't done some things that make me feel priggish and self-righteous rather than face an alternative that I know my father would have disapproved of.

If I noticed ominous symptoms while working in the yard, I wouldn't consider it kvetching to call the doctor. On the other hand, my attitude toward kvetching is so much of a standing joke in my own family that if my daughters are complaining about something they provide my response before I can open my mouth: "I know, Daddy—'Pull up your socks.' " Our daughters were both born after my father died. They grew up in New York rather than the area Jacob Schiff assigned us to. A year after my father died, we bought a Village brownstone of the sort whose price had made my father go dark behind the eyes, and we still live there. (My father would have thought, at least, that the house was connected to an appropriate Village literary figure: according to the guides who show tourists around the Village, a huge sycamore in our backyard whose branches extend into a courtyard next to our house is the tree O. Henry had in mind when he wrote "The Last Leaf.") When my daughters were growing up, I had the luxury of spending a lot more time with them than my father had been able to spend with me. I didn't have to be a grocer. If I take a long car ride with one of them, there is a lot of talk, but not much of it is terribly personal. I suppose I could argue that my responsibilities in that area are not as obvious as they might be if one of our children were a boy or if they didn't have the sort of mother who is cherished for her heart-to-hearts even by people who are not related to her, but the truth is that I'm only marginally better at that sort of thing than my father was. Some of the messages I've tried to get across to my children may still be in code. I'm not sure if I can isolate the theme of their upbringing, but I know that I didn't want it to be as different from my upbringing as it seemed to be on the surface. Sometimes I think that the theme I had in mind was "Despite all evidence to the contrary, you are being raised in Kansas City."

I still sometimes speak, I know, as if I'd never left Kansas City myself, despite all evidence to the contrary. Alice refers to that custom as my Kansas City Act. There are ways in which I probably still think of Kansas City as the norm against which everything else must be judged. In our family, the use of Kansas City as a sort of moral compass is sometimes expressed as if it were a time zone—Kansas City Mean. Part of the reason for the existence of Kansas City Mean, I suppose, is that Kansas City is intertwined in my mind with my father and the messages he sent me. It's also true, as I once wrote, that for Midwesterners who have come to New York "a home town has no statute of limitations: If a Wall Street trader who grew up in Des Moines says late in the evening, 'I better be getting home,' he may be talking about a co-op apartment on East Seventy-first Street, but if he says after a day that included an expensive down-tick in automotive issues and a visit by a couple of men from the SEC, 'Sometimes I think about going home,' he's talking about Des Moines, Iowa." I've never stopped discussing Kansas City barbecue or the Kansas City Blues. Even the phrase "lose less" remains active in our family, unconnected to gin rummy. If Alice and I are taken to dinner at a restaurant whose pretensions obviously exceed its skills, the explanation for ordering the simplest item on the menu is understood: lose less. Once, for my sins, I found myself about to participate in a symposium entitled "The Writer as Conscience of the World," and my announcement to Alice that I intended to say as little as I could get away with took the form of "I believe I will approach this situation as Phil Horowitz might have approached it."

Would my father think that the Grand Plan had worked out more or less as devised? I've always assumed that I'm at least in one of the fields he had in mind—or in one of the fields that were acceptable as fallbacks once it became clear that I was not going to be the President of the United States. It's also possible, of course, that, wanting to believe this, I've given, say, that summer of typing school some significance that was never really there. Before my father died, I was already more interested in writing about America—particularly America between the coasts—than in writing about anything else. When I went back to New

York from Kansas City the summer he died, I had trouble getting started again on the sort of long reporting pieces I'd been doing for *The New Yorker*. The then editor, William Shawn, encouraged me to try a series we had previously discussed—a three-thousand-word piece from somewhere in the United States every three weeks. I did that for fifteen years, any number of times reporting a story from some place I had visited on those long car trips across the country. What more appropriate beat could a real American have? Twenty years or so after my father died, I began doing a verse once a week for *The Nation*, just as he had once done a verse every day for the menu at Trillin's. In a book I did on my experience of writing verse about the events of the day—it was called *Deadline Poet*—I began one chapter, "You might say that I come from a poetic background."

I've always thought of my father as having accomplished what he set out to do, but, of course, children go through life seeing their parents in terms of themselves: he accomplished what he set out to do for Sukey and me. I suppose someone could add up the facts of my father's life and come to the conclusion that he was an unfulfilled man. There were, after all, plenty of immigrants of his era who made privileged Americans out of themselves rather than their sons or daughters. He was happy in his family but he never had the pleasure of work that truly satisfied him. He never had a crack at California. I'd like to believe, though, that he didn't think in those terms. I'd like to believe that he thought more in terms of what Rabbi Hadas called a sense of continuity. I've felt his presence most intensely at those landmarks of continuity—on the day, for instance, when each of my daughters graduated from Yale. But I can often hear his voice in mine, and not just when I'm asking for a translation of "The left-handed lizard climbed up the eucalyptus tree and ate a persimmon." I hope my daughters can hear it, too.

RUSSELL KAUTZ
ST. JOSEPH, MO.

"You might as well be a mensch."